THE ROAD WE WALK ON

WALK ON

Navigating Life with Joy

Janene Zirges

Dedication

I dedicate this book to my mom, Lucille Ziegenbusch, and mother-in-law, Kathleen Newman, who are both in eternity with Jesus experiencing the fullness of joy and His pleasures forevermore.

And to my Lord and Savior, the source of all my joy and hope.

Let the Journey Begin

"You make known to me the path of life;

in your presence there is fullness of joy;

at your right hand are pleasures forevermore"

Psalm 16:11

The last load of laundry was finally folded and put away. The travel bags were back in storage. The car was emptied of all the travel games, puzzles, and books. It had been nearly a week since we pulled into the driveway in the dead of night, ending our memorable three-week journey to the other side of the world. At least traveling across ten states from California to Indiana seemed like the other side of the world to three energetic kids, two to seven years old. Soon everything would be back to the usual routine, back to work, and back to finish the school year. Yet we talked about the trip for weeks, looked at pictures, and recalled the fun, difficult, and crazy things that happened along the way.

It was the destination that prompted us to plan a trip to Indiana - a visit to see my aging grandpa for maybe the last time, and to show my kids the places I explored when visiting as a child. But, although the destination was important and full of memories, the journey there was also valuable. From the planning stages to the side trips, the return trip to the unpacking, the entire journey was filled with memories and lessons. Isn't that how all of life is? Why do we rush through life without hardly taking a second glance? We occasionally will slam on the brakes to glance at a few key moments, but we often fail to see these things for the joy that God has intended for them to be. Life is not only about the destinations but also how we journey on life's road.

What is your destination? Graduation? Career? Marriage? Retirement? Those are the scenic views or pit stops, if you will, along the road of life en route to our final destination, heaven. How often do we focus so narrowly on each destination that we miss the beauty of the view and the instructive opportunities God provides along the way? If the destination were merely all that mattered to God, why does He not take us to Heaven as soon as we accept His gift of salvation? Yet that was never God's intention. Some may have a longer journey than others, but we all have a road to travel.

When I began writing this book, various titles came to mind. *Enjoy the Journey* was the first. The more I wrote, however, the more I realized our journey in life will not always be enjoyable. God intends for us to live a life of joy regardless of how bumpy or treacherous the road is. Paul reminds us to "Rejoice in the Lord always, I will say it again: Rejoice!" (Philippians 4:4). Joy is an attitude, a quality, and not merely an emotion or a happy feeling which depends upon our circumstances. Joy should, in fact, be expressed by our deep commitment to God because of our faith and trust in a sovereign God who promises to always be there even in difficult times. R.C. Sproul states,

"We might suffer all kinds of painful setbacks and afflictions, but those things should not rob us of the foundational joy we have in Christ. We can rejoice in all things because everything else is insignificant compared to the wonderful relationship we enjoy with our heavenly Father through the work of Christ on our behalf."[1]

According to the *Westminster Shorter Catechism*, "Man's chief end is to glorify God and to enjoy Him

---

[1] *Everyone's a Theologian* by R.C. Sproul. Copyright Ligonier Ministries 2014. Used by permission of Ligonier Ministries. All rights reserved.

forever."[2] The attitudes we have as we walk through life will either be attractive to others or offensive. Living a life of joy regardless of the circumstances is what will draw others to Christ, not a life of misery and complaining. "…whatever you do, do all to the glory of God" (1 Corinthians 10:31b). Therefore, God desires for us to live a life of joy because it brings honor and glory to His name. While part of this book is about how we can take an active part in making the journey more enjoyable, ultimately to live a life of joy is a calling on the road of everyday life regardless of the circumstances we may face. And then, when our journey one day comes to its end, we will experience true, unfettered joy in the presence of our Lord and King forever!

The biographical stories, personal accounts, and Biblical truths in this book will help to illustrate how walking the road with joy is possible. We will recount the stories of Noah trusting God's timing and Abraham relying on God's provision. I share Joseph's story as his faith was unwavering even when his life was turned upside down, and Paul, who in the face of persecution and imprisonment, could not stop rejoicing in the Lord as he encouraged the

---

[2] The Westminster Shorter Catechism, 1646 and 1647 by the Westminster Assembly.

church to do the same. And these are but a few of the stories I will tell of how God's people through the centuries have trusted and found joy on the road set before them.

The following chapters are also dotted with my personal family stories and those of friends and acquaintances. This book was born out of areas in my own life in which I was convicted, and while writing, God worked me through the process of bringing more joy into my own life and living out what I knew I should. I have not arrived, it is still a daily process, but God has taught me so much through this. The principles in *The Road We Walk On* are lessons I wish I had been taught and encouraged to live out when I was a goal-oriented mom, often too busy and driven to enjoy the blessings I had, and to experience joy even in the trials rather than grumbling and complaining. My hope is that this book will touch the hearts of those seeking practical ways to find joy regardless of where they are on the road.

Do you know where you are going or what stage of the journey you are on? What are the destinations you have planned out for your life? Do you even have a plan, or know what kind of traveler you are? We will begin by considering how wandering aimlessly is not conducive to a genuinely joyful life.

"For we are his workmanship, created in Christ Jesus for good works, which God prepared beforehand, that we should walk in them" (Ephesians 2:10).

God has a master plan for each of us. He has ordained our days and He wants us to have purpose in life. Planning is not some evil device to drive us crazy or create stress, instead, it should be the opposite, bringing peace and contentment. Once you know what your destinations are, you can focus on the importance of preparation at each step of the journey. We will talk about why being prepared will affect our attitude toward both the planned and unplanned events in our lives, because we know there is a good chance there will be detours along the way. Going forward in life without preparation could lead to disaster. We see in the book of Proverbs that "The plans of the diligent lead to profit as surely as haste leads to poverty" (Proverbs 21:5).

Having a plan and being prepared does not mean life will be boring drudgery. On the contrary, God still desires for us to enjoy the scenic routes in life, to experience the beauty and wonders of His creation, and the joy of being in relationship with Him. He also desires for us to find rest for our souls, as He provides the much-needed rest stops along life's road.

Life is not always smooth sailing, and we will all face roadblocks and detours at one time or another. We will delve into why the road we travel is marked with trials, define what trials are, and then how we can navigate them. We will also explore how we travel from dark tunnels and find safe harbors. When you look at your path, do you see stumbling blocks or steppingstones? Do you sometimes even wonder if you are there yet? We have many choices along this road, including the people we choose to travel through life with, and we will discuss how those choices affect our attitude of joy. We will talk about identifying and dealing with the excess baggage and dirty laundry we collect while on life's journey, recognizing how sin steals our joy.

When we come to the end of life's road, will we be known by others to have lived a life of joy? What kind of life traveler are you? Be encouraged, for no matter where you are going or how far you have come, there are countless opportunities to soak in all of life's marvelous details. Together, let us explore the beauty of navigating a life of joy on *This Road We Walk On*.

When God sets His plan before me,

I'll go with joy and bring Him glory.

Even when the road is steep,

With difficult turns and waters deep,

I will trust your plan through the triumphs and trials,

For your joy is my strength as I travel the miles.

And may it be said when my days are thru,

I walked the road with a heart of joy

because I hoped in you.

One

The Destination

"All the days ordained for me were written in your book
before one of them came to be"
Psalm 139:16

I had seen Grandpa Ramsey only once since my
wedding, when he and Grandma came to California after
the birth of their great-granddaughter, Sarah. Grandma's
long-term memory was already showing signs of failing on
this trip. Less than two years later, she was gone from us
and home with Jesus. Now Grandpa was alone, and I
wished to see him one more time before he was only a
memory, too.

I later came to realize my grandpa's life was a
beautiful example of how to live a life of joy. He had an
easy-going manner, a gentle smile, and a faith that was
unwavering. He lived through two world wars, the
Depression, and countless changes in the world around
him, yet he still managed to have a heart full of joy whether

he was tinkering in the garage or meeting his great-grandchildren for the first time.

I had wanted to show my husband and children where I spent several of my childhood summers. The time seemed right for us to make a family trip to Indiana. The destination had been chosen—the first step in the journey.

Do You Know Where You Are Going?

Before you can go anywhere, you must first know what your destination is going to be. The destination may appear to be at the end, but really it is the beginning. Without a destination, there is nowhere to go. Some trips are in the works for years. Maybe it's a dream vacation you hope to take when you retire; or when you were a child, your family set out on a vacation to visit far-off relatives.

Since I am now a grandma with most of my grandchildren out of state, I have had this urge to travel often, because I don't want to miss out on too many milestones; or hugs and snuggles and laughter! Then there are the unexpected trips—the unscheduled business trip, a family emergency, or the urgent request of a friend. Some destinations we choose with much excitement and others are chosen for us. To arrive at the intended destination requires a journey, and an expectation to get out on the road.

We are all on a journey as we go through life, and many of these journeys over the centuries have been documented in biographies and narratives. We read of hundreds of journeys in the Bible alone. Christ's life here on earth was a journey, despite being quite different from our own. He lived a perfect life as fully God, while also experiencing everything we experience as He was also fully human. It is this perfectly balanced life that made redemption on the cross even a possibility. As Christians, we have a final destination in heaven because Christ made a way for us to get there. Until then, however, our journey is here on earth and each of us has a different road to travel.

Sometimes, don't you just wish God would lay out the map and say, "You are here [X], and this is where you are going [X], just follow me and the path will be easy?" At what point would we begin to trust the map more than the map maker? If a storm comes and washes out the road, we may find ourselves lost and confused. Landmarks change, timing changes, circumstances change, and our hearts change, but God's compassion, presence, and faithfulness are constant. God does have the map, He has the master plan, but He does not reveal it to us all at once. Therefore, not one of us knows how long our journey is or exactly where the road will take us.

Nevertheless, God still invites us to be a part of choosing our direction and being involved in the planning and preparation. Whenever we have planned a family vacation, we found that if the kids, especially the older ones, participated in the decision-making process, they were filled with greater excitement and expectancy for the trip ahead. In this same way, we should be excited to discover the places in life that God will take us. Like the much-anticipated vacation, God wants us to look forward to what lies ahead.

The following principles may seem simple and maybe you are confident in your goal-setting skills, but for the teen or young adult who might be reading this, these strategies will lay a firm foundation for your future. Even if your journey has already taken you many places, I hope you can still glean encouragement from this chapter. My husband and I have recently become empty nesters, and we are now resetting some of our goals. What does God have for us now? A need for a career change, retirement, or a death in the family are all circumstances that may give us pause to ask the question, *what now?* Every new chapter in our journey requires a fresh look at what lies before us.

Time to pull out the binoculars and gain some perspective. We never stop making choices while we are on this road of life. So, with that said…

What Are Your Goals in Life?

We are given many opportunities to choose our destinations in life. Some are daily choices—*do I go to the store,* or *do I visit a friend?* Others are life-altering, and very possibly once-in-a-lifetime choices. For example, *who will I marry* or *what career path should I take? Is God calling me to the mission field?* Each of these questions we will likely ask ourselves at one point or another in our lives. Much like the expectancy of an upcoming vacation, we look forward to traveling the road which takes us to our destinations in life.

Anxiety can creep in when we are unsure where life is taking us or become concerned if we have made the right choices. Conversely, when we know we are going in the right direction, peace is our companion. And how do we know we are going in the right direction unless we know where our ultimate destination is? Here is what is most comforting—God already knows your destination. Psalm 139:16 reminds us "All the days ordained for me were written in your book before one of them came to be." Joy comes when we allow God's Spirit to lead us.

Are you wandering aimlessly, or do you have purpose?

Although God has ordained our days, He has still given us the gift of free will. With our free will, we are given the opportunity to make choices about where we are going on our life's journey. If you wish to find joy in the journey, knowing where you are going is essential to the planning and preparation for what lies ahead. God has placed each of us on this earth for a purpose. He has plans for us. Are we willing to follow them?

Let me clarify—the occasional, spontaneous adventure can be a joyful and worthwhile experience. Taking a drive to nowhere in particular can sometimes be especially freeing. Only be sure the drive is not on a cold and rainy night, or you might find yourself stuck in the middle of a bog. Even if we don't have the exact location pinpointed, we are still making choices about which road to take, which direction to go, and when to begin.

So How Do We Choose?

What direction do you want to go? As children, most of us are taught by parents, teachers, or adults who cross our paths the very basics of decision-making and how to form wise choices. We are confronted with dozens of choices each day. But how do we go about making the bigger choices in life, the ones which will have a lasting impact on how well the journey is ultimately traveled?

Make A Wish List of Goals

What are your grandest dreams? If there were no limitations to what you could do, where would you like life to take you? Don't hold back even if they seem out there. "Delight yourself in the LORD and He will give you the desires of your heart. Commit your way to the LORD; trust in Him and He will act" (Psalm 37:4–5). Although it seems likely some dreams may take a lifetime to accomplish, and not every dream will be fulfilled, God's purposes are often accomplished by men and women who were willing to pursue a dream. When Paul committed to preaching the Gospel, the Jews rejected his teaching, and his plan took a detour. Instead, Paul's desire sent him on a journey to the Gentiles in Asia, which God used to spread the Gospel to the far corners of the earth.

Has God given you the heart to work with children? Then maybe your destination is opening a daycare center, working in an orphanage, or being a schoolteacher. Or is it possible God is calling you and your spouse to adoption?

God may have given you an aptitude in science or medicine, as He did Florence Nightingale, the founder of modern nursing, or Hudson Taylor, the founder of China Inland Mission, who served in China as a doctor and missionary most of his life. In that case, the road may lead you to be a missionary doctor, or to conducting research into the cures of horrific diseases. Your calling could be a hospice volunteer bringing comfort to the sick and dying, or faithfully serving as a nurse or doctor in your local community. God may even be calling the country boy to become an itinerant pastor because of his earnest desire that everyone in his township know Jesus.

Paul reminds us that God has prepared each of us to do something with our lives; "For we are his workmanship, created in Christ Jesus for good works, which God prepared beforehand, that we should walk in them" (Ephesians 2:10). God sometimes reveals His plan in small steps, and at other times He reveals a grander view. And for us—we are to step out onto the path as He reveals it to our hearts.

Make A List of Essentials–What Do You *Really* Need?

Dreaming is a valuable exercise in keeping us from becoming too near-sighted, but we should also make a more practical list of our present and future needs.

Everyone will usually list the basics of food, shelter, and clothing, but what about the intangible necessities? Are you someone who needs people around encouraging one another, or giving and receiving hugs? Does your heart burst into a joyful song when you walk into a room full of people? Then you will likely want to pour your life into a community or church which offers a variety of social activities.

Are you a more solitary soul, where your dearest companion is a cup of coffee on the back patio, with the whisper of the breeze in the trees? If you have come to realize this is more your style, but your work environment is a chaotic busy mess, you may want to consider a career change where you are allowed plenty of thinking time, possibly working on your own rather than with a team.

What do you believe will satisfy your most heartfelt needs? A word of caution, however. Don't ever get too comfortable because God will most likely stretch you just as you settle in for the ride. But we are certain of this—God has made each of us with differing needs spiritually and emotionally. The decisions we make and the paths we choose in life can have a significant impact on whether those needs are met. God has created each of us with diverse, and often, unique skill sets, personalities, strengths

17

and weaknesses, gifts, and talents. We cannot all do the same job, live in the same place, doing the same things. That would be boring and unfulfilling. God is a creative god who made us all different on purpose. Yes, we are made in His image for the purpose of bringing Him glory, but He also wants us to discover how He has created each of us as individuals to do the good works He has planned for us to do.

For you created my inmost being;

you knit me together in my mother's womb.

I praise you because I am fearfully and wonderfully made;

your works are wonderful,

I know that full well.

My frame was not hidden from you

when I was made in the secret place,

when I was woven together in the depths of the earth.

(Psalm 139:13-15)

Prioritize

Organize both lists of goals and dreams in order from short-to-long-term, then choose the ones you hope to pursue first. Think of this as the road map for your life. Each goal is like a rest stop on the highway, or maybe a historical point of interest. Every goal has a purpose and is to be enjoyed and appreciated. One goal may build on a previous one. We don't want to focus too far ahead, or we may miss the beauty of all that is in between. But without our long-term goals, we will find ourselves stuck in a rut with nowhere to go.

Let's say you had a goal of visiting every baseball stadium in the country within five years. Your goal is to visit all thirty of them, but you will certainly want to enjoy the adventure and excitement of visiting them while also witnessing the spectacular plays, the crack of the bat and cheers of the crowd, and especially the smells of freshly cut grass mingled with a juicy hotdog slathered in mustard.

Therefore remember, knowing your destination is significant to making your life's journey joyful and fulfilling. If you are traveling in the darkness without a map or plan, who knows what you will run into? It may not be very pleasant. Keep your sights on the first goals on your list and each one will come into focus as you travel along the road.

"Let your eyes look straight ahead, fix your gaze directly before you. Make level paths for your feet and take only ways that are firm. Do not swerve to the right or the left; keep your foot from evil" (Proverbs 4:25–27).

Pray

"Commit to the Lord whatever you do, and he will establish your plans" (Proverbs 16:3). Pray and ask for discernment to be sure your plans are God's plans. This does not mean trying to persuade God to go in our direction. On the contrary, we need to be sure our plans conform to God's plans. "In his heart a man plans his course, but the Lord determines his steps" (Proverbs 16:9). Remember God has the aerial view of the whole journey, while we can only see a limited distance ahead. He reveals what we need to know and prepares us for each step along the way.

If we choose to follow an alternate path from the one God has mapped out for us, we may be placing our lives at risk of traveling in treacherous territory. "There is a way that seems right to a man, but in the end it leads to death" (Proverbs 16:25). The Psalms are filled with requests seeking God's guidance and direction, such as in Psalm 25:4, "Make me to know your ways, O LORD; teach me your paths." We would be wise to follow David's example here, to always be praying our goals and plans are in step with God's plans for us.

Plan

Now you can begin planning your objectives for reaching your stated goals. For our trip to Indiana, there was much we hoped to see along the way. So, we made a list of all the places we wanted to go—Focus on the Family while in Colorado Springs, the Laura Ingalls Wilder House in Mansfield, Missouri, the St. Louis Arch, and President Lincoln's Boyhood home. As it turned out, we also experienced an April blizzard, torrential rains, and an unscheduled trip to the emergency room. However, our careful planning turned the unexpected into fantastical adventures and lessons of faith, rather than disasters of great peril. It is good to remember, "The plans of the diligent lead to profit as surely as haste leads to poverty" (Proverbs 21:5). We will discuss further planning in the next chapter.

Re-Evaluate Your Goals on a Regular Basis

Remember, our ways are not always God's. We make our plans, but as we travel along the road, we may encounter roadblocks, detours, or scheduling conflicts. Are you aware that a plane's navigation system is always adjusting with the shifting wind currents to stay on course? And when there is turbulence from a storm or a mechanical failure, the pilot will take over control to safely navigate through or around the obstacle. Are there times when we would love to just put our day on autopilot? Absolutely! However, as we navigate through life, we must remain vigilant and be prepared to adjust to changes in the landscape. Look over your list of goals monthly, quarterly, and/or semi-annually, and ask yourself, am I staying on course and maintaining focus on my objectives? Am I reading my map and continuing to move in the direction God wants me to go?

Reevaluating our goals and adjusting is essential if we hope to arrive at our desired destination. Again, we should be praying when we are unsure, or have roadblocks and detours ahead of us, asking for wisdom and discernment as to which direction He intends for us to go next. Ultimately, our primary goal is to bring glory to God in all we do, or there will be no joy when we arrive.

Why in the world is all this goal-setting necessary to live a life of joy? Because the first step to finding joy on this road of life is to know where we are going, for without a destination we simply end up wandering aimlessly through life. To know where we are going, we should establish goals that are aligned with God's plans and prioritize and pray about them. Then we can begin planning our objectives for reaching those goals, reevaluating them on a regular basis. Once we have our destinations in view, we can begin preparing for the exciting adventure that lies before us.

I wonder where this road is going,
I really do not like not knowing.
Why should I wander aimlessly,
And maybe miss what I should see?
Some goals I should begin to make,
Then I will know which road to take.
For when I know to where I'm going,
My heart has joy upon the knowing.

Two

The Preparation

"Trust in the Lord with all your heart and lean not on your
own understanding; in all your ways acknowledge him
and he shall direct your paths"
Proverbs 3:5-6

One day, as I sat on the shore of a lake watching my
youngest son fish, I was intrigued by a couple preparing to
go out on the lake. Each had rolled their own kayak to the
shore's edge. For fifteen minutes they prepared to enter the
water by removing the wheels, checking to make sure
everything was securely fastened down, and arranging their
poles. Apparently, a good deal of diligence had taken place
before they ever arrived, the evidence being their proper
fishing gear and first-rate equipment. Finally, once they
were certain all was ready, they launched out onto the
gentle waters glimmering in the warm sunlight, and glided
effortlessly to their destination, the middle of the lake.

24

They hoped all the meticulous preparation would translate into a safe trip out on the lake, with a successful bounty of fish by day's end.

Some consider preparation a necessary evil, others believe it to be a tedious waste of time, while others are energized and filled with anticipation as they organize and prepare. So, why is all the preparation necessary? Can't we just go, throwing caution to the wind–what difference will it make? Because, how we prepare can mean the difference between a miserable journey and an enjoyable one. Even a trip to the grocery store requires a bit of planning.

Shopping without a prepared list can be dangerous for many of us. We can end up spending more than we should because we buy items we hadn't intended to buy. And of course, we all know one should never go to the grocery store on an empty stomach! Whatever the destination, a minimum amount of planning is required, for some more than others. Even a spontaneous adventure needs some preparation. Usually, the better prepared you are, the smoother the trip is along the way.

How Do You Plan Your Journeys?

Are you an organized planner with lists and maps; or are you a carefree planner, you know—the plan as you go—spontaneous type? As we packed for a camping trip one weekend, I didn't have as much time as usual to check our supply tubs. Sure enough, when we sat down to eat our first meal, there were no utensils! Now, I am usually a meticulous planner, creating detailed lists and timelines, but for some reason, as we prepped for the trip, checking the camping tubs never made the list. Fortunately, we were camping with our church, and many were willing to provide us with the necessary utensils, sparing us the embarrassment of eating like Knights of the Round Table!

My misstep made for a funny memory, but what if we had not been prepared in other ways? On this particular trip, the temperatures dipped into the mid-40s as soon as the sun sank behind the ridgeline. What if we had not checked the weather conditions and had only packed shorts and t-shirts? We would have been very unhappy campers, indeed! Like unprepared kayakers, *we'd be up the creek without a paddle.* Do you know what the definition of this little idiom is? —A challenging or troublesome situation, especially one that cannot be easily resolved. Improper planning can sometimes lead to disastrous results. In the same manner, life has a way of getting chaotic and uncomfortable when we do not try to plan for the future or even our daily activities. God desires for us to be prepared.

There are many examples of preparation in the Bible. For decades, Noah prepared the ark for a flood no one believed was coming. God prepared the way for the Israelites to leave the captivity of Egypt and occupy the Promised Land. The Israelite kings regularly prepared for battle. Solomon followed God's instructions in preparation for the building of the temple. Nehemiah prepared for the rebuilding of the city walls. John the Baptist prepared the way for Christ's ministry.

Jesus said, "Let not your hearts be troubled. Believe in God; believe also in me. In my Father's house are many rooms. If it were not so, would I have told you that I go to prepare a place for you? And if I go and prepare a place for you, I will come again and will take you to myself, that where I am you may be also" (John 14:1-3). Why prepare? Because God places high value on preparation.

So, who needs a map, anyway?

Maps are a valuable resource for any vacation, particularly if you are traveling to a place you have never been before. These days maps come in all forms: paper maps, computer-generated maps, and the map app on your phone. A map contains useful information needed to tell us which way to go, what obstacles to avoid, what we will see along the way, and even an approximate time of arrival.

27

Some travelers are navigationally challenged, and a map is their lifeline for survival out on the road.

For others, the map is merely a guideline they check just to be sure they are going in the right direction. In whatever way you use a map, having one is an essential tool for an enjoyable journey. If you choose to go without one, hopefully, you have the fortitude, the daring nature of the early pioneers, and a really good compass! Otherwise, you may find yourself in places you never intended.

The funny thing about maps though, is that if you keep a stack of them in your glove compartment but never take them out, they are virtually useless. If the GPS is never turned on, it won't be able to direct you to your destination. We have an excellent map available to us, to give us direction in life—the Bible. The problem is, we often leave it unopened on the shelf or the coffee table, not able to heed its advice.

The Bible is God's map to us, giving direction in our lives. Many of us have grown up hearing Psalm 119:105, "Your word is a lamp to my feet and a light to my path." We can think of the Bible as our GPS for life, "God's Providential System" which illuminates the path He has set before us. We can consult the map of God's Word at every turn to be sure the roads we take are leading us to the desired destination.

Seek the Advice of Those Who Have Gone Before

When we planned our trip to Indiana, we asked others who had been there before, such as my parents, what were the best routes and what we could expect to encounter along the way. We were able to glean from their experience and choose from the safest roads, the most scenic, or the swiftest highway. From others, we learned what historical sites we might enjoy discovering and unusual places we might take pleasure in seeing.

Our seven-year-old daughter, Sarah, was absolutely captivated by the Little House on the Prairie stories by Laura Ingalls Wilder, and someone had told us about the Laura Ingalls Wilder House in Mansfield, Missouri. That slight detour was quickly added to our itinerary and it became one of the highlights of our trip. Tour books are useful but talking to someone who has actually been there is even better. They can describe the sights and sounds of Lincoln's Boyhood Home or Squire Boone's Cavern in a way in which no tour book possibly could.

We would be wise to seek counsel and advice in our life's journeys as well. Proverbs 15:22 reminds us, "Plans fail for lack of counsel, but with many advisers they succeed." Who can you go to when you need some direction in your life or when you are facing a difficult road in front of you? God gives us parents, spouses, pastors, teachers, mentors, grandparents, and friends, to name a few. They can provide a wealth of knowledge while guiding us to move in the right direction and help us avoid a hazardous route as we make significant life choices.

The most successful kings surrounded themselves with wise and learned men and sought their counsel and advice when important decisions needed to be made. Make sure, however, you seek the advice of Godly men and women who can give you trustworthy guidance. "So you will walk in the way of good men and keep to the paths of the righteous" (Proverbs 2:20).

Pray About It

Ultimately, though, our direction should come from God. We want to seek His advice through daily prayer and meditation. When we do, He will use His Word, the advice of wise counsel, and the experiences of others to guide us through the roads of life. When we faithfully put our wholehearted trust in God's direction, acknowledging His ways rather than our own, He will help bring us to the desired goal.

Does this mean if we follow all these steps our plans will never fail? Of course not! Not everything will go as intended and in a later chapter we will discuss how to deal with unexpected changes to our plans. When Dwight D. Eisenhower recalled his turn as commanding General of the Allied Forces, he stated, "In preparing for battle I have always found that plans are useless, but planning is indispensable." In other words, everything may not go as planned; however, failing to plan is just the same as planning to fail.

So how does planning and preparation translate into a joyful journey? If we are anxious about our future, taking pleasure in life's everyday joys will be difficult. And why are we anxious? Maybe because we have failed to adequately plan, making the future seem as though we are traveling on a dark, windy road with no signs. What joy is there when we are consumed by worry about what is around the corner? Ultimately, we can trust our future to God and His plan for our lives, but He still expects us to do our part and plan by way of His guidance and instruction.

"For I know the plans I have for you,' declares the Lord, 'plans to prosper you and not to harm you, plans to give you hope and a future" (Jeremiah 29:11 NIV). This was a promise given by God to the people of Israel while they were in exile. Although not a direct promise to us today, this is a picture of God's character in sovereignly fulfilling His plans for those who are faithful to Him. My children heard me say many times "God has great plans for you," and He does, for each of us. He will not, however, just hand those plans to us on a silver platter. It is our responsibility to pursue those plans, and then we can find joy in our journey because we know God's plans for us are secure.

Sometimes I really do not care,
To know the how, just tell me where.
But when the map I fail to follow,
The journey will seem lost and hollow.
I know that I should plan my days,
And trust that God will guide my ways.
For when the road is clearly seen,
A joyful journey I will glean.

Three

Off the Beaten Path

"This is what the Lord says: 'Stand at the crossroads and
look; ask for the ancient paths, ask where the good way is,
and walk in it, and you will find rest for your souls"
Jeremiah 6:16

Did you know that if you only travel on the main
road around the Grand Canyon, you will see only a slight
portion of the grandness of the canyon itself? Oh, you
might get a glimpse here or there, but you will not likely
see the vastness or the majesty of God's handiwork. We
don't want to miss those scenic turnouts along the road.
Some of the most spectacular views can only be seen if you
actually pull in and stop for the scenic vistas. As we travel
through life, we do not want to miss those special moments
God gives along the way, and we may need to be reminded
of the greatness of God. The same God who created the
vastness of the universe is the same God who cares about

every detail of our journey and how we travel through it. God is sovereign in all things.

There are times when God wants us to push past the boundaries of our comfortable path, to see the adventures which are beyond the borders of the same predictable scenery. To me, adventure has always had an element of joy and excitement. Sure, there can be a little bit of scary mixed in, but how will we ever be stretched if we are not willing to take the less traveled road from time to time? Are we willing to look over the edge a little? This doesn't mean we climb over the safety rails and carelessly put ourselves in harm's way; but if you stand back too far, you will not see how the deep green waters of the river play hide and seek between the cliffs of the canyon below or how effortlessly the eagle's nest hangs in the cleft of the towering canyon wall.

Then there are the designated rest stops along the road. God desires for us to rest in Him, either to refresh us after a difficult part of the journey or to be sure we are prepared for struggles that may lie ahead. When we are rushing through life, we are either too busy to notice all God is doing in our lives or we are too exhausted to focus on the things which truly matter in our journey. What special qualities could we be missing in our children, spouse, friends, or loved ones because we are quickly going from one activity to the next? What opportunity for ministry or blessing are we neglecting because they are in the way of our own plans? Most of us do not travel along the physical road in reckless abandon, risking life and limb, so why do we sometimes travel through life that way?

What God desires is that on occasion we stop and take pause. Psalm 77:12 reminds us, "I will consider all your works and meditate on all your mighty deeds." And Psalm 46:10 says, "Be still and know that I am God." The road was never meant to be traveled without stopping. Here are three reasons we should expect to stop and take pause: to catch the view; to take advantage of rest stops; and to evaluate our course. Great men of God, such as Abraham, Moses, David, and Paul all did these things. Jesus even told Martha to slow down and sit at His feet as Mary did.

Catch the View

Whenever traveling through a beautiful countryside or exploring all the wonders of God's creation this world has to offer, we would be remiss if we did not take the time to pull off the main highway and onto the scenic paths. When we do, we find ourselves amazed by the beauty and majesty stretching out before us. How often do we take the time to appreciate God's creation, or for that matter, the many details of our lives that He is orchestrating by His mighty hand? Job was confronted with the same question in discourse with his friend Elihu, "Hear this, O Job; stop and consider the wondrous works of God. Do you know how God lays his command upon them and causes the lightning of his cloud to shine?" (Job 37:14-15).

Job was reminded to reflect on an all-knowing God whose works are awesome in majesty and power. How often do we stop and take pause to consider the power He has over the universe, yet He is so intimately involved with all of creation and our existence, He not only holds the heavens in place but each of our individual lives, as well. Therefore, the reason we take pause—enjoying the scenic view—is to reflect on God's wondrous works, to become intimately aware of all God has done, so as we travel along the road, we do not forget He is the source of our existence.

Reflecting on God's wondrous works means acknowledging God's sovereign power, which then also means getting to rejoice in His sovereign plan for our lives. When we don't stop to reflect, we forget who is ultimately in control and life becomes a hectic treadmill instead of a joyous and beautiful journey.

Abraham was also given the opportunity to take a pause and reflect on God's faithfulness. "The Lord said to Abram after Lot had parted from him. "Lift up your eyes from where you are and look north and south and east and west. All the land that you see I will give you and your offspring forever...Go, walk through the length and breadth of the land, for I am giving it to you" (Genesis 13:14-15,17). In the verses prior to this passage, Lot took what he wanted as if he deserved it. On the other hand, Abram, who trusted God's promise, willingly let Lot take what appeared to be the choicest land, and God provided for Abram abundantly. God's promised provision was authentic and everlasting.

Sometimes, on our journey, we need to stop and *survey the land*, to take stock of God's provision in our lives, recognizing, "that which God has to show us is infinitely better and more desirable than anything that the world has to offer in our view"[3]. God's provision does not only include material possessions, but health, salvation, and family, such as our spouse or children. Do we spend too much time being irritated by our children or our spouse's weaknesses, rather than focusing on what makes them

---

[3] Matthew Henry Commentary, Pg. 28.

special and unique to us and to God? Take time to appreciate the precious gifts from God that they are.

Secondly, Abram was not only blessed, but he was to be a blessing, both then and to future generations. Are there opportunities for ministry or the blessing of others we may be missing or even neglecting because we are plodding forward with our own plans? If we never pause to see the beautiful view God has placed along the journey, how are we to see these things? When we trust God for His provision and appreciate the family and friends God has put in our life, all while seeking to serve Him, then there is greater potential for us to walk through life with confidence and a bounce in our step. Stop for a moment and take time to survey your landscape, offering a prayer of thanks for the blessings God has placed on your journey. And ask yourself, how can I bless someone else's journey? How can I expand my view?

Rest Stops

How often has your determination to reach a certain destination caused you to drive *straight through*? Resolved to reach the goal, we will sometimes travel without rest until we arrive—and when we get there, we are exhausted and completely spent. Then we are left with an extra day of recovery from that final push. Is this how we travel through life sometimes—always pressing? God's plan was not for us to go barreling down the road with no time to rest. On the contrary, He desires for us to find refreshment for both body and soul.

In the first week of earth's existence, God placed a priority on rest when after six days of creating everything from the land and sea to the plants and animals, and culminating with Adam and Eve, He rested. This week-long endeavor is something that would be exhausting for any mortal. God, of course, does not get exhausted, but by His example, we learn the importance of rest. If even the infinite and amazing God of the Universe takes the time to rest after work, even when He did not need it, how much more should we embrace the gift of rest that He created? In Exodus, God commanded the Israelites to take a Sabbath rest. A day to cease their labors and focus on the faithfulness of God by worshiping and honoring him. God not only designed the Sabbath for His honor but also for our benefit.

Jesus tells us in Matthew 11:28, "Come to me, all you who are weary and burdened, and I will give you rest. Take my yoke upon you and learn from me, for I am gentle and humble in heart, and you will find rest for your souls.

For my yoke is easy and my burden is light." Christ offers us rest for our souls. He will take our burdens and give us a yoke that is much lighter. "Rest for the soul is the most desirable rest. The only way, and sure way to find rest for your souls, is to sit at Christ's feet and hear His Word"[4].

Practical application of this may come in the form of quiet times, personal retreats, or reflection days with longer periods of meditation and prayer sitting at the feet of Jesus and learning from Him. And, yes, setting aside our sabbath day each week to give glory and honor to the One who brings us rest. When we are refreshed and rested, we will likely experience more joy in our daily journeys.

Staying Within the Boundaries

On the one hand, God instructs us to remain on the path He has set before us, but, on the other hand, He wants us to survey the land, to explore the landscape. Clearly, there are boundaries, fences, and "No Trespassing" signs we should consider when exploring off the beaten path. God provides boundaries for our protection much like the guard rails at the edges of the canyon. They are a reminder that what is on the other side, though sometimes beautiful,

---

[4] Matthew Henry Commentary, Pg. 1262-1263.

is a treacherous path that will most likely result in a devastating fall.

God set boundaries for His people when they entered the promised land. The boundaries were set to keep invaders out of the land but to also make a clear distinction between His people and the ungodly. God places boundaries for each of us individually as well. My boundaries will not be the same as yours because we each have a different path to follow.

When I set off for college, my upbringing and profession of faith helped to set clear boundaries for many of the life choices I would be faced with. Unfortunately, during my first three years of college, I basically ignored the boundaries of righteous living and common sense, and fell into partying and drinking, looking for enjoyment on a dead-end street. Overstepping those boundaries resulted in two extra years of college to make up for failed classes, and a trunk full of emotional baggage for choices I could never take back.

The ill-chosen detour did not bring me joy, only temporary pleasures, and unwanted consequences. I eventually fell into despair, but in His mercy, God brought some important people into my life who nudged and sometimes shoved, me back onto the right path and within the boundaries of God's plan for my life. One might say those three years were wasted, but I am grateful God used those mistakes in my life to teach me incredibly valuable lessons.

The fence around the hazardous waste dump is there to protect us from being contaminated by the things which will make us sick or even kill us. God's protective fences from the contamination of this world are His commandments and precepts, beginning with the Ten Commandments He gave to Moses for the people of Israel to follow. His boundaries are clear—do not worship any other Gods, do not worship idols or take His name in vain, honor the sabbath, honor your parents, do not murder, do not commit adultery, and do not steal, do not bear false witness or covet what is not yours. Over thousands of years of kingdoms and empires, those boundaries remain firmly in place.

Many rulers and scholars have tried to alter or ignore them but doing so ultimately led to chaos and the demise of many a nation and people. Failing in even one of these commandments leaves a breach in the fence which makes us vulnerable. He didn't give those commandments to be a killjoy, to make life miserable. On the contrary, He gave them out of compassion, to protect His people from the death and destruction that sin and rebellion bring. Sometimes we look over the fence with the "No Trespassing" sign and think, it is so beautiful over there or it looks like they are enjoying life more than I am. This is when we need to trust God's perspective is better than ours, and that those boundaries are there to protect us from the unforeseen dangers on the other side of the fence.

How Do We Know When We Are Off Course?

The people of Israel had chosen the wrong path over and over again. God finally said, "STOP!!" "This is what the Lord says: 'Stand at the crossroads and look; ask for the ancient paths, ask where the good way is, and walk in it, and you will find rest for your souls'" (Jeremiah 6:16). Sometimes God wants us to stop and evaluate the paths we have chosen. We can ask ourselves: 1) Are we on the *ancient paths*? In other words, are we following the example of those who have wisely gone before us? 2) Are we walking in the *good way*? Some before us have chosen to walk in evil ways, while others have chosen the good way.

Which example will we choose to follow? When we follow in the footsteps of godly men and women who have gone before us, we will find *rest for our souls*.

Consequently, if you are finding yourself anxious, unsettled, or lost, then it's time to stand at the crossroads and take a good look at where you are going.

When traveling, one way of keeping on course, especially when we are in unfamiliar territory, is regularly consulting our map. However, there are times when we may misread the map or ignore the map because we think another way is better, faster, or easier. Our map for life is God's Word. Psalm 119:105 bears repeating, "Your word is a lamp to my feet and a light to my path." Did you know there are over eighty verses referring to paths or ways? Do you think maybe God is concerned about our journey and what direction we are going?

We all stray from the beaten path at times, requiring a course correction of our actions or attitudes. Sometimes we need minor adjustments, like setting your phone aside before you get sucked into social media because you promised your five-year-old you would do a puzzle with him. Maybe you struggle with unhealthy eating habits, or with making poor movie or TV choices. At other times we need a tow truck to bring us back onto the main highway because we are stuck in the mire and clay of some destructive behavior or attitude.

How do we make those adjustments? The first step is to recognize and admit we are off course; "If we confess our sins, he is faithful and just to forgive us our sins and to cleanse us from all unrighteousness" (1 John 1:9). Then we must turn around! "Repent, then, and turn to God, so that your sins may be wiped out, that times of refreshing may come from the Lord" (Acts 3:19). The further we drift from God the easier it is to wander down the wrong path. If you have only strayed a short distance from the main road, it should be a simple task to put on the brakes and turn around. However, if you have traveled far from the path God intended for you to follow, you may need roadside assistance.

Thus, God provides the help to get back on course, whether coming from a pastor, friend, parent, teacher, or the prompting of the Holy Spirit. "The way of a fool is right in his own eyes, but a wise man listens to advice" (Proverbs 12:15). "Listen to advice and accept instruction, that you may gain wisdom in the future" (Proverbs 19:20). Don't be like the traveler who is unwilling to ask for directions even though they may be terribly lost. Instead, be willing to be accountable to God and to others, to listen to correction and advice when given.

Always Keep Your Compass with You

God has a plan for each one of us, yet only He knows where the road will take us. We can trust His compass and the tools of navigation He has provided for us; His Word, prayer, wise counsel, and prompting of the Holy Spirit, to make sure we are staying on the right path. The path may seem unclear, but if you are continually checking your compass and trusting in God's guidance, He will keep you going in the right direction. At times He even wants us to slow down and catch the view, not missing the beauty and joy this life has to offer.

God may also want us to take a rest from the long journey, especially when the road becomes difficult or dangerous. There will be days when we need to come in from the storm and take refuge. And when we stray too far, God will bring us back, either gently or firmly, but once we are His, He will never allow us to be lost forever (John 10:27-29). Eventually, we will find the path again, but what joy, what opportunity might we miss when we stray out of God's plan? Therefore, keep your compass with you when you explore the wondrous joys of this journey, so you will remain within the boundaries of His perfect plan.

Instead of taking time to see
the wondrous plan God has for me,
I sometimes rush through life each day,
and then I fail to stop and pray.
Yet when I'm weary I should rest,
then go along the road that's best.
Lord help me when I dare to stray,
renew my joy upon the way.

Four

Roadblocks and Detours

"Many are the plans in a man's heart,
but it is the Lord's purpose that prevails"
Proverbs 19:21

Have you ever gone somewhere and right when it appears the trip is going smoothly, suddenly the traffic stops! You then find yourself traveling at a snail's pace. As you approach the flashing yellow lights, you notice a sign which says, "Bridge closed, detour ahead." We were faced with that very dilemma on a trip one Thanksgiving to my sister's in central California. The kids were excited to get to see their cousins, but we started our trip later than planned. With the travel already holiday-heavy, what normally took 4 ½ to 5 hours ended up being an eight-hour ordeal.

It would be wonderful if every time we went somewhere, whether a trip to the grocery store or a well-deserved vacation, the road was clear…no construction, no weather delays…only clear sailing from start to finish! On

48

most occasions these trips are uneventful, but from time to time we are faced with one that does not go exactly how we planned. And as much as we would like there to be clear sailing all through life, this is not what we actually face. We can plan to our heart's content and yet still face unexpected obstacles that seem to take us off course or delay our plans.

So how do we handle the detours and roadblocks appearing to stand in the way of experiencing joy? If God intends for us to have joy in the journey, why doesn't He make the road less bumpy, and with fewer obstacles? First, let's try to understand why roadblocks and detours even occur. Here are four main reasons why our travels through life do not go as expected or planned:

1) The results of a sinful world affect both the godly and the wicked.

2) The consequences of poor choices or sin: God's correction.

3) God's protection or way of leading us in a different direction.

4) The testing of our faith or for displaying God's glory.

When a roadblock or detour is placed on our path, one or more of these will be the reason for the trial.

Discerning which one in particular, can impact how we walk through the trial.

Let's look at these one at a time.

The Results of a Sinful World Affect Both the Godly and the Wicked

From the time of the fall every man and woman has been corrupted by sin and the earth has been subject to the curse of sin. When Adam and Eve sinned, God brought a curse upon the earth allowing natural disasters and the sin of mankind to affect any of us. Genesis 3:17-19 says, "Cursed is the ground because of you; through painful toil you will eat food from it all the days of your life. It will produce thorns and thistles for you, and you will eat the plants of the field. By the sweat of your brow you will eat your food until you return to the ground".

Also, we are all born with a sinful nature and our sins not only affect us but also the lives of others around us. Because of God's infinite grace and mercy, He did not destroy everything and start over but instead provided a way of redemption through His son, Jesus Christ. Yet, throughout history, mankind and all of creation have been affected by the results of sin and no one is exempt.

Job was a righteous man before God, yet in his seemingly smooth journey, he abruptly began to face innumerable trials and troubles. Why? What did he do to deserve such suffering? Because the rain falls on the just and the unjust, alike. Yes, God allowed Job to be tested by Satan, but much of his suffering was the results of circumstances that were completely out of his control because we live in a world affected by sin. Through the course of time, earthquakes and floods, tornados and hurricanes, famine and disease do not single out the wicked and the unrighteous. Instead, we all have the potential for disaster to touch us in some way.

Neither can we hide in seclusion or live in a bubble. We can do our best to stay free from sin and its resulting consequence, but someone else's poor choices may impact each of us because none of our sin happens in a vacuum. I have often told my children their choices not only affect them but will also affect all those around them. It is, therefore, safe to assume the choices others make will impact us as well. There are countless lives lost resulting from drunk drivers who make foolish choices with no regard for who would be impacted by their decisions.

Attempting to be righteous before God will not free us of the effects of sin, it will only give us the strength to endure when we travel through life. And because life is meant to be traveled, we cannot live in total seclusion thinking we can keep the coming trials at bay. The effects of natural disasters and the consequences of other people's sins–these are beyond our control–but be assured they are not out of God's sovereignty. What is in our control is how we respond to those trials.

The Consequences of Poor Choices or Sin: God's Correction

Suppose you are traveling through the Rockies or the High Sierras. Wisdom would dictate traveling through certain mountain passes at a particular time of year would not be advisable. You have a choice to make–travel the recommended highways, or go your own way, ignoring wise counsel and sound judgment. With the latter, you might get away with poor decisions for a little while, but sooner or later you are more than likely to be faced with mud slides, rockslides, or ice and snow. What you thought was the better way becomes dangerous or impassable. You are faced with the consequences of your decision; admit your mistake and turn back. What if your poor judgment results in injury of yourself or those who are traveling with you?

Which brings us to the choices we do have and when our trials or difficulties are the consequences of poor choices or sin. This will eventually result in God's correction. We expect the wicked to get what they deserve, yet at times we may forget even the sins of the righteous man must still be paid with the price of death or its consequences (Romans 6:23). We are given the gift of grace because of Christ's sacrifice on the cross, but we are still subject to God's discipline and correction. Grace does not give us the license to sin (Romans 6:1-2).

There are numerous examples in the Bible and in our own lives that illustrate how much God will not tolerate sin. For instance, the sinful events involving David and Bathsheba in 2 Samuel come to mind. David was a man after God's own heart, yet he still faced choices to obey or to sin. In this case, he coveted another man's wife, saw to it her husband was killed, and conspired to cover up the transgression. Now do you suppose because David had God's favor, he should have been free from any consequences? Of course not, and neither did God!

Nathan the prophet exposed his error in judgment and told him what the price would be. David acknowledged his sin, asked for forgiveness, and accepted God's discipline. The price? The life of his newborn son. Do you think maybe the death of his son got his attention? We may not experience consequences as harsh as this, but we are all going to face some sort of consequences through trials and discipline. This is not to say we won't experience grace, but grace comes to us at God's discretion and not through any negotiating on our part.

Proverbs 3:11-12 explains it this way: "Do not despise the Lord's discipline and do not resent his rebuke, because the LORD disciplines those He loves...." God cares deeply about the condition of our hearts, and He knows we cannot experience joy in our lives if we are mired in sin or if poor choices impede our journey. God's correction and discipline is the most loving action He can take to get us back on the right path of finding joy again.

God's Protection or Way of Leading Us in a Different Direction

There will be times we are faced with a trial or difficulty because of God's grace and protection or His way of leading us in a different direction. At the time we do not see this as a blessing, yet we discover hours or maybe even years later, God allowed the roadblock or detour, and we were either protected from disastrous results or given a blessing even greater than we had hoped. "Have no fear of sudden disaster or of the ruin that overtakes the wicked, for the LORD will be at your side and will keep your foot from being snared" (Proverbs 3:25-26). Though often difficult, we can trust in God's timing, because only God knows what treacherous ground lies ahead which may have caused the delay.

How many times have you left for work later than you planned because of a phone call or an uncooperative child? And maybe you later discovered if you had been at a certain intersection at your usual time, you could have been involved in a serious accident. Coincidence, a stroke of luck, or God's grace? As many of the victims' stories of the September 11, 2001 terrorist attacks unfolded, there were also the accounts of those who missed those ill-fated flights because of traffic, failed alarm clocks, or last-minute plans. At that moment, I would imagine some of them were frustrated or angry, having their plans altered, until only one or two hours later they discovered what horrible disaster could have taken them.

Then there are the times God is leading us in another direction. We make our plans, but God chooses the results. My husband left his job in 2007 because he felt God was prompting him to do so even when we weren't sure where He was leading us. He knew changes were needed as he foresaw the impending downfall of our national economy, and believed it was a prudent decision for our family. What we didn't anticipate was a few months in, we still had no outside income, no insurance, and we almost lost our house. After examining our hearts, we determined this didn't happen because of sin in his life or poor choices, but because of God's timing.

Before all this happened, Phil had anticipated early retirement and more opportunities to serve in ministry. Some of what my husband had wisely saved for retirement, would become our emergency fund. We could have fallen into the depths of despair, but instead, we accepted the tenuous circumstances as an opportunity to trust that God had a better plan. As a result, the nine months Phil was out of work were some of the sweetest times of growth and closeness to God our family had ever experienced. As we waited on God, our complete reliance on Him through all the difficulties we faced brought tremendous joy despite the circumstances.

God met each need, through our friends and church community, side jobs, and anonymous gifts. He was our steadfast provider. Then God opened the door to a new job my husband would never have thought to apply for a couple of years before. God used his new sphere of influence in incredible ways and helped him to discover and utilize skills that were rarely used in his previous employment. Sixteen years later he is a leader in his industry and God has expanded his influence as an ambassador for Christ.

One of my favorite narratives from the Bible is the life of Joseph. Here was a young man full of promise and ambition. He had confirmation from God he would one day rule even over his own family. But little did he know the many detours he would face in his journey from know-it-all little brother to second in command of all Egypt. The fact that there are thirteen chapters in Genesis dedicated to the recounting of Joseph's life story demonstrates how important this story was to God, and that He hoped lessons could be gleaned from it. What can we learn from Joseph's bumpy yet colorful journey?

Joseph was easily his father's favorite, having been born to Jacob's beloved wife, Rachel, in his old age. His father bestowed upon Joseph special gifts, the most prized being his multi-colored tunic. A gift of this significance was usually reserved for the first born. At seventeen, Joseph went with his older brothers in the fields to tend the flocks and would report to his father when those brothers misbehaved. He was not so beloved by his brothers, instead, their hearts began filling with hatred and resentment toward him.

When Joseph tattled on his brothers, he did not help his cause. And then there were the dreams. God gave Joseph a dream which placed his brothers in submission to him through the analogy of his brothers' wheat bundles bowing down to his. A second dream of celestial bodies bowing to Joseph had even his father submitting to his authority. Sounds good, right? Not to his brothers, and they hated Joseph even more because of this.

As Christians, this is a reminder to not get too smug in our own righteousness. A difficulty may come into our lives for more than one reason. If we need an attitude adjustment or a sinful behavior to be corrected, God may use a trial as a way of discipline. Yet, God may also use this same trial to accomplish His purposes and in Joseph's case, to fulfill the promise of a nation that would one day be God's chosen people. What came next, many would argue, was partly his own doing, but was also part of God's plan.

And here is where the unexpected twists and turns began in Joseph's unusual journey. In their jealousy, some of Joseph's brothers sought to kill him, but God had other plans, and instead, Joseph's brothers sold him into slavery.

Let's not forget the confusion and devastation Joseph must have felt from the betrayal of his brothers. They later admitted they could hear Joseph's distress when he begged them for his release. However, at the time his brothers did not listen, and he ended up in Egypt, of all places, sold into the household of Potiphar, the captain of Pharaoh's guard.

We are told God gave Joseph success and he found favor in his master's sight, becoming chief overseer of his household. All seemed happy and life appeared good, until Potiphar's wife slanders Joseph's good character, falsely accusing him of improper advances. And just like that, Joseph finds himself in a predicament and thrown in jail. Once again, God gave Joseph success even while in prison and he interpreted the dreams of two of Pharaoh's officials. Yet for two more years, Joseph languished in jail—forgotten.

Not until one of the officials remembered him, was the purpose of God's plan set into full motion. The Pharaoh had two bizarre dreams of seven plump cows devouring seven skinny cows, and seven juicy ears of corn swallowed up by seven scrawny ears of corn. From jail to the throne room, Joseph now stood before Pharaoh who implored him to interpret his dreams. One wonders if Joseph somehow sensed this was more than just an easy ticket out of jail, but more so to fulfill a grander plan God had for him. Joseph could have taken the credit for his gift of interpretation, but he rightfully acknowledged God to be the true interpreter of the dreams.

If you know the story, you know the dreams meant there would be seven years of plenty, followed by seven years of famine in all of Egypt. And Joseph, through the wisdom God had given him, was the one who came up with the ingenious plan to save Egypt when the famine materialized. For thirteen years Joseph went through the valleys of abandonment, obscurity, accusations, and misunderstandings, and each time he somehow made the best of a difficult situation, rising in favor and responsibility.

God used those years to train and prepare Joseph for the responsibilities which would one day be placed on his shoulders in Pharaoh's court. As we travel our own peaks and valleys, do we ever consider God might be preparing us for what is ahead? God always has a plan and purpose. He is always preparing us for something.

But here is the intriguing part of the story—Joseph saved his father and brothers, and their families from certain starvation because Pharaoh had placed him as second in command. He had been given authority over them for a purpose! After all that Joseph had been through, he could have become a bitter, angry man. In spite and revenge, he could have chosen to let his family, whose descendants would one day be the Children of Israel, simply waste away and suffer their own fate.

Joseph did test his brothers before revealing to them who he was, with a bit of teasing and taunting; I did not say he was perfect. But in the end, Joseph rejoiced at the reunion with his brothers and the joy brought to his father. Though he may have not fully understood, Joseph trusted God's plan and God's timing. After his father's death Joseph truly realized God's purposes, for he told his brothers, "You intended harm to me, but God intended it for good to accomplish what is now being done, the saving of many lives" (Genesis 50:20).

Whether the detours and roadblocks we face are God's protection or a way of leading us in a different direction, of this we can be sure, "And we know that in all things God works for the good of those who love Him, who have been called according to His purpose" (Romans 8:28). In this we can rejoice, for even when our journey doesn't go according to our plan, we can always trust God has a perfect plan.

The Testing of Our Faith or for Displaying God's Glory

Finally, along with correction, protection, and a fallen world, one important reason we face detours and roadblocks is for the testing of our faith or for the displaying of God's glory. What is perplexing for many unbelievers is witnessing the joy and resiliency of a Christian going through a difficult time and becoming stronger in his or her faith. The unbeliever expects the Christian to accuse God and lose heart and is dumbfounded when he does not.

Even Christians, at times, question God, and this may be the very reason we are tested. God desires for us to grow in our faith. If we never faced a trial, if life never took a detour, we would become complacent. We would stay in the same place and not go anywhere. God allows us to be tested from time to time to keep us fighting the good fight and recognizing God's hand in everything.

One of my favorite verses in scripture is James 1:2-3, "Consider it pure joy, my brothers, whenever you face trials of many kinds, because you know that the testing of your faith produces perseverance." The Greek translation in this instance of the word "trials" (*peirasmois*) refers to difficulties coming from external circumstances, rather than the consequences we face from being tempted by our sin nature which comes from within.

True trials of this kind are not considered a punishment, but instead an opportunity to rejoice in what this testing will produce. We may not be joyful *for* the trial, but we should be joyful *in* it and *through* it. The word "face" can also be expressed "fall into" as in the potholes we cannot avoid, but we can drive through and endure what may result from it. But how can we find joy in that?

James tells us we know the testing of our faith produces endurance. Like pure gold which withstands the refiner's fire, so should pure faith endure regardless of how hot the fire is through the trial. And Paul tells us in Romans 5:3-5, "…but we rejoice in our sufferings, knowing that suffering produces endurance, and endurance produces character, and character produces hope, and hope does not put us to shame, because God's love has been poured into our hearts through the Holy Spirit who has been given to us." We are to be steadfast and to endure in the face of trials because of the hope it eventually brings.

Abraham is an incredible example of perseverance and the resulting joy despite one of God's most difficult tests: the sacrifice of His son. God Had proven himself trustworthy time and again. In His covenant with Abraham,

God had promised a son followed by many decedents to him and Sarah. Even though Abraham had faltered at times in his obedience to God, he finally saw the promise of a son fulfilled. Abraham enjoyed years of fellowship with God; therefore, he may have been perplexed when God requested he take his beloved son of the covenant up the mountain and offer him as a sacrifice. It is likely he did not fully understand the test, and the journey up the mountain must have been difficult, but he trusted God.

His attitude going up the mountain may not have revealed any anger, discouragement, grumbling, or complaining, because there appeared to be no worry or fear in Isaac. Therefore, when God revealed His plan to Abraham through the provision of a sacrificial ram, he was rewarded for his faith, and he worshiped God. And unbeknownst to Abraham, his example of faith and perseverance through a seemingly cruel trial, would stand the test of time, along with giving future generations a glimpse of what God the Father would do to redeem the whole world through the sacrifice of His own son, Jesus Christ.

God also wants us to search for the answers to the hard questions so that when we find them, we can share them with others. This brings us to the other part of the equation. When we are tested and persevere, God's glory is displayed to the world. Consider the blind man Jesus encountered. He was asked whose sin had caused the man to be blind. "Neither this man nor his parents sinned," said Jesus, "but this happened so that the work of God might be displayed in his life" (John 9:3).

Why did Mary and Martha face the unbearable sadness of their brother's death when Christ could have easily healed him before he died? So God could reveal His glory in Christ raising him from the dead. Why was Peter imprisoned? So God could miraculously release him, and God's glory be displayed. Souls are brought to Christ because they see God work in the life of faithful Christians. Sometimes the road to a desired destination is arduous or difficult. Sometimes the travel is uncomfortable or long, but once we arrive, what we view with our eyes, the joy we experience, it is all well worth it. The beauty of God's grace is worth the trials, and God is glorified when we persevere.

What causes us to desire to travel to places like the Grand Canyon, the Swiss Alps, or the English countryside? Why are certain destinations appealing? Usually because of the accounts and glowing descriptions of those who have gone there before. Our friends tell us how lovely their trip was, how much joy they had in going. Therefore, we may desire to go because we want the same experience. In the same way, those around us should know that although the road we travel in life is not always easy, it is definitely worth it.

There may also be times when we find ourselves on a narrow precipice with nowhere to go. When our oldest son was barely a teenager, he and my husband embarked on the quest to climb Mt. Whitney in California. They were both in great physical condition and the hike itself was challenging but not overly strenuous. They went with a group of men from the church who spent months planning and preparing. Their date to climb in mid-September was chosen by lottery. The temperatures can fluctuate that time of year, and they were prepared, arriving at base camp to relatively mild temperatures and beautiful skies.

However, they had not expected the weather to turn so drastically, temperatures dropping and the winds kicking up. They would discover later it was the worst weather day of the season. Yet the men were undaunted by the challenging task before them. My husband and son began their 22-mile trek in the dark of night in order to arrive at the top of the mountain at the ideal time of day. The wind was biting, but the layers of clothing, their boots, gloves, and hats were keeping the freezing temperatures from becoming unbearable. They came to a critical junction on the trail taking a break before their final ascent to the peak. Here they made a disappointing discovery—their water supply had frozen.

It would no longer be safe for them to take the trail without water. They prayed and reasoned through their options and decided their only choice was to turn back, short of their desired goal. Then the unexpected happened! Descending around the bend of the mountain a hiker appeared who had decided to cut his climb short because the 50 mph winds had whisked away his only head covering. He said he overheard their radio communications and then pulled out an unfrozen water bottle hidden deep in his jacket. His unselfish gift meant they could continue their quest to the top.

One obstacle was overcome, yet the rest of the hike still had its challenges. In fact, they soon came upon a narrow portion of the trail, only wide enough to take single file. On either side of the path were steep ravines. On a normal day, this part of the path is difficult at best, but with the freezing temperatures and high winds, it was venturing on the impassable. But they were determined to make their way to the top. So down on their hands and knees they went, keeping a low profile until they reached the cleft of a rock on the other side.

Now with only a couple miles to go and a renewed resolve, they methodically ascended the rest of the trail up the mountain, reaching their goal. There was celebration in the small hut on the summit, but not much time to linger before heading back down the mountain as the temps dropped into the teens. The trip back down was long but uneventful. When they reached the bottom of the Whitney Portal, they asked around about the hiker who had given them his water. It seemed no one else had crossed his path, nor did he return to the portal. No one was ever reported missing.

An angel? Maybe. But whoever he was, when my husband and son were faced with an obstacle they didn't see coming, God provided a way for them to continue on the path to their destination. God has also used their experience and the stories which followed to teach many lessons over the years. Lessons of perseverance, prayer, trust, protection, and provision. All these lessons were now imprinted on their hearts, not because the road was easy and carefree, but because they faced challenges that were necessary to overcome in order to learn the lessons well.

There is no getting around the fact we will face trials; we will experience hardship in this life. But our joy comes in knowing God is sovereign, He has plans for us. Although we do not see what is coming around the bend, God does, and He will guide us through the twists and turns of life's road. However, it is important to remember God usually intends for us to go through the trial, not around it. Which is how we grow stronger in our character and how we grow deeper in our relationship with God. And that is all the reason we need to consider it all joy when we face trials of many kinds!

When detours seem to hinder the way
and trials appear to frustrate my day
A heart of joy I wish to know,
an attitude of trust I will show.
When life doesn't seem to go as it should,
I'll remember He works all things for good.
And so I choose to rejoice each day,
even though the journey may not go my way.

Five

Roadside Assistance–Getting Back On Course

"Because he loves me," says the Lord, "I will rescue him;

I will protect him,

for he acknowledges my name. He will call upon me,

and I will answer him;

I will be with him in trouble"

Psalm 91:14-15

When we are on the road and faced with a detour, we can allow our emotions to get the better of us. We can get caught up in the moment and become frustrated with the situation. This, in turn, leads to impaired judgment which could bring disastrous results. Trials in our lives can also cause stress which can strip away our joy. We become so focused on the difficulty of the trial, we fail to see the good that God will bring or the lessons we can learn. How does a flat tire impact our plans? What happens when your flight is delayed, and your plans must be altered? What is our attitude when our destination is changed? Sometimes our plans are so set in stone that when those plans are altered, the pleasure of the trip is spoiled.

We are living in challenging times—this is nothing new—there have been challenging times throughout history. And by challenge, I mean for Christians and people of faith, when the lines between good and evil are blurred. When the clear path doesn't seem to be in focus anymore, we tend to veer off into questionable territory. Sometimes, it is not so much that our choices are sinful, just not wise. When we make decisions out of character with God's plan or purpose in our lives, then there is a greater possibility we will face obstacles and detours we hadn't expected. As God's children, He will eventually redirect us back to the intended path.

Learning to ride a bike is a rite of passage. We watched as each of our children tried to negotiate a straight line down the driveway or across a bumpy campsite. They overcorrected a dozen times until a single wobble would send them into oblivion or leave them sprawled on the ground. Most of the time they learn through trial and error, and we should let them. They may end up with a few scrapes and a little humility, but hopefully, build enough confidence to go it alone.

Would we be good parents if we let our child wobble too far off the sidewalk and into oncoming traffic? NO WAY!! We would yell, block their path, or use whatever means possible to keep them from harm. God, in His mercy, does the same thing for us. In life, He allows us opportunities to learn and try new things. He also expects we will make mistakes, get scraped up, and eventually try again. Whether knowingly or not, sometimes our choices can throw us out into traffic, and God compassionately places a roadblock in our path.

Why is this important? Because, in our instant gratification world, and a world that exalts perfection and frowns on failure, we often forget to be grateful for the difficult lessons which teach us and mold us. It is not failure to ask for help, instead, it is a blessing that God is there with us and for us. Remember that every situation we face is ultimately about God's glory and reputation. God can bring healing through the tears or show us His mercies in the trials. When we face a roadblock or detour, we have a choice, either push God to the side of the road, or draw near to His presence and accept the assistance and refuge He provides. How is God going to use your circumstance for His glory?

Sometimes we get so caught up in the obstacles, the struggles, and the hard path, that we are unable to focus on the growth which is taking place, the faith, and trust being built. Like a cyclist training for a race, sometimes the road to victory—or just getting in the race—requires hard work, sacrifice, and perseverance. As a former athlete, I know when the training becomes drudgery, when there is no joy in the hard work, then the victory is not as sweet.

Let's face the facts: God said this life path will have places of suffering along the way. No detour will remove it for us. At times, we have no other choice but to follow the bumpy road, take the long way around, or climb the steep arduous hill in order to reach our destination, God's intended destination for each of us. Wouldn't you rather travel that difficult road with joy, than with complaining? Grumbling only makes the road harder and takes our focus off the goal.

We should also remember, we are not the only ones suffering and struggling, or faced with difficulties and challenges. Sometimes an entire community suffers because of a natural disaster, the foolish decision of a drunk driver, or an economic downturn. If an entire country is steeped in political turmoil and division, it eventually trickles down to many of us as individuals, families, and communities, thereby affecting our livelihoods, our safety, our relationships, and our ability to worship and serve God.

Therefore, how we deal with disaster, calamity, and trials, not only impacts us personally, but can have a broader effect on those we work with, worship with, and influence daily. You may think to yourself, *I don't have any influence,* or *I am not that important.* Oh, but you are! Your decisions influence, or at the very least, affect, many of your interactions on a daily basis.

How Should We Respond to Roadblocks and Detours?

Why do we often respond to the roadblocks and detours in our lives as bothersome and frustrating? Could it be a reminder we are not in control? Remember when we talked about how important planning and preparation is to know where we are going? Though this is vital, ultimately, God is the only one who truly knows what lies ahead. Here is where we learn to trust God to direct us through difficulties that come along the way.

It is through the guidance of the Holy Spirit that we can discern why we are going through the trial and how to best travel through it with joy, finding ourselves stronger for it on the other side. To do this, we can first decide if the roadblock is a result of a fallen world and circumstances which are out of our control, such as natural disasters or someone else's sin; or could it be the correction for our own sin or poor choices? And if not for these reasons, then for God's protection or God's way of testing our faith and bringing Him glory.

This brings us back to the importance of our relationship with Christ and being in tune with His Spirit. If we are in God's Word, seeking His will, and humbly going before Him in prayer daily, then it is much easier to discern which of the above circumstances may have brought these roadblocks and detours into our path. Paul reminds us in Philippians 1:9-10, "And this is my prayer: that your love may abound more and more in knowledge and depth of insight, so that you may be able to discern what is best and may be pure and blameless until the day of Christ." Paul was a remarkable man who, by example, lived a life of joy regardless of the circumstances. His journey on this earth took some very unusual twists and turns, yet he never wavered in his pursuit of sharing the Gospel with joy and eagerness.

Before his conversion he no doubt knew what a life of affluence and wealth was like. He hobnobbed with the wealthiest of the priest and Pharisees and was quite powerful and influential in his own right. Yet once he found redemption in Christ, that is when he experienced true joy, despite being imprisoned on numerous occasions, caught in a vicious storm, shipwrecked, stoned and left for dead, run out of town after town, bitten by vipers, and hated by his former associates.

Paul came to understand the difficulties we face in life are all a part of God's plan and we can rejoice in them because they bring growth. Remember the verse from Romans—"suffering produces perseverance; perseverance, character, and character, hope" (Romans 5:3-4). Then verse 5 reminds us that "hope does not make us ashamed, because the love of God has been poured out into our hearts through the Holy Spirit, the One having been given to us" (Romans 5:5, Berean Literal Bible). In our suffering, God gives us hope, which is a reason to rejoice.

Paul also knew the importance of having a grateful heart and expressing his gratefulness to God. "Rejoice always, pray without ceasing, give thanks in all circumstances; for this is the will of god in Christ Jesus for you" (1 Thessalonians 5:16-18). Even if life is hard, we still have plenty of reasons to be thankful and grateful for all of God's promises and gifts He has bestowed up us.

God created a marvelous world for us to live in, and He has given us salvation through the sacrifice of His son,

Jesus, and the forgiveness of sins. He has given us His Word for instruction and encouragement, and He has given us the guidance and comfort of the Holy Spirit. We have no excuse but to walk the road with grateful hearts. I try to practice a heart of thankfulness each day, expressing my gratitude toward God when I rise in the morning and before I go to sleep. I have discovered experiencing joy comes much easier to me when I also express gratefulness even for the small things.

> "Behold God is my salvation; I will trust, and will not be afraid; for the LORD GOD is my strength and my song, and he has become my salvation. With joy you will draw water from the wells of salvation. And you will say in that day: Give thanks to the LORD, call upon his name, make known his deeds among the peoples, proclaim that his name is exalted. Sing praises to the LORD, for he has done gloriously; let this be made known in all the earth" (Isaiah 12:2-5).

If we are faced with roadblocks or detours, it is usually easy to tell when they are circumstances beyond our control such as earthquakes, tornados, drunk drivers, sickness, or disease. Yet if none of those situations show up on our radar, then next we can ask ourselves, are our trials a result of our poor choices? Am I sensing a conviction of the Holy Spirit because of unconfessed sin in my life? "Search me, O God, and know my heart! Try me and know my thoughts! And see if there be any grievous way in me, and lead me in the way everlasting!" (Psalm 139:23-24).

Might I need to admit I am in the act of a transgression and this trial is the consequence of that sin? Am I facing the consequence of a poor choice because I did not seek wise counsel or refused to listen to it? The saying *confession is good for the soul* is a truism and exactly what God requires for us to live a life of joy. Psalm 51 is a beautiful psalm of David's confession after committing adultery with Bathsheba.

"Have mercy on me, O God, according to
your unfailing love; According to your great
compassion blot out my transgressions.
Wash away all my iniquity and cleanse me
from my sin... Let me hear joy and gladness;
let the bones you have crushed rejoice...
Create in me a pure heart, O God,
and renew a steadfast spirit within me.
Do not cast me from your presence
or take your Holy Spirit from me.

Restore to me the joy of your salvation

and grant me a willing spirit to sustain me"

(Psalm 51:1-2, 8, 10-12)

David realized the burden of unconfessed sin would crush his spirit and hinder his relationship with God. And with that, there would be no joy. Therefore, when we acknowledge our sin, the weight of the resulting consequences will not crush us, but we will instead have our joy restored and our relationship with God renewed.

If we can confidently determine the trials we are facing are not a result of living in a sinful world, and we have examined our hearts and confessed the sin in our own lives, then we can ask God what He might be trying to accomplish through the difficulties we are encountering. If the bridge is out, then the detour signs are there to protect us from falling into the river. Is it possible God may be protecting us from potential danger? An accident up the road or exposure to a harmful situation. Or is God trying to move us in a different direction in life?

Maybe the layoff from a job happens because two months down the road God has an even better fit. The trial could be something God is using to build our character or increase our faith. Ask God to reveal what He wants you to learn, and where He wants you to grow. Keep your heart open to the instruction of the Holy Spirit. But let me be clear, it is important to recognize we may never fully understand, this side of heaven, why we are faced with a particular trial. A present trial could be something we will not have answers to until God chooses to reveal His glory.

We might also keep in mind that the roadblocks we are facing could be the result of more than one of the above circumstances; a chronic illness or disability can be a result of the fall, but it may also be something God uses to bring glory to Himself. In fact, because God *works all things for good*[5], if we respond to our trials with the proper attitude then every detour or roadblock has the potential to bring God glory.

Roadside Assistance

If you have consulted God's Word and spent time in prayer and you are still having difficulty determining what circumstances brought about the roadblock you are facing, then the time has come to seek wise counsel and advice. "Let the wise listen and add to their learning, and let the discerning get guidance" (Proverbs 1:5). Sometimes what we cannot see from within is easily discernable to someone with an outside point of view. It is all a matter of

---

[5] Romans 8:28.

perspective. We may only see a short distance down the road, but someone who has just been there may be able to give you a clearer understanding of why the detour is needed.

Remember that God has an aerial view of the whole landscape! There are several Proverbs in which God encourages us to seek wise counsel. "The heart of the discerning acquires knowledge; the ears of the wise seek it out" (Proverbs 18:15). Yet even after prayer and counsel, this ultimately comes down to trusting that God has our best interest at heart and believing that if He has allowed a difficulty on our journey, then He will also provide a way for us to walk through it.

Once we recognize the circumstances, we are better able to evaluate how we might face and walk through a trial. On this journey, we are given the ability to call on "roadside assistance," to call upon God, and the assistance of others to help us navigate the road hazards we encounter on the way. According to Proverbs 27:12, to go forward without assistance would be a foolish endeavor, as "the prudent see danger and take refuge, but the simple keep going and pay the penalty." God does not require or wish for us to go it alone. He has sent a helper, our *parakletos,* the Holy Spirit! He is our comforter and counselor who comes alongside us to aid and assist us whenever we need help. God also provides family members, friends, pastors, mentors, teachers, and sometimes even strangers to help guide us when the way seems difficult, dark, or just a little foggy.

Ecclesiastes 4:9-10 reminds us that "two are better than one, because they have a good return for the work: if one falls down, his friend can help him up. But pity the man who falls and has no one to help him up." It is not weakness to call upon God for help, in fact, He says "I will rescue him; I will protect him, for he acknowledges my name. He will call upon me, and I will answer him; I will be with him in trouble" (Psalm 91:14-15).

Step by Step

In order to experience joy instead of frustration, discouragement, or anger, there are steps we can take:
Acknowledge God's sovereignty; He is in control:
"The mind of man plans his way, but the LORD directs his steps" (Proverbs 16:9).
"I know, O LORD, that a man's life is not his own; it is not for man to direct his steps" (Jeremiah 10:23).
Remember God's unfailing love for us and His faithfulness:

"Because of the LORD's great love we are not consumed, for his compassions never fail. They are new every morning; great is your faithfulness" (Lamentations 3:22-23).

Give our burdens to God; as Christians, they are His to bear:

"Praise be to the LORD, to God our Savior, who daily bears our burdens" (Psalm 68:19).

"Cast your cares on the LORD and he will sustain you; He will never let the righteous be shaken" (Psalm 55:22).

"Cast all your anxiety on Him because He cares for you" (1 Peter 5:7).

Bring your requests before God with a thankful and rejoicing heart despite the circumstances:

"Rejoice in the Lord always. I will say it again: Rejoice! Let your gentleness be evident to all. The Lord is near. Do not be anxious about anything, but in every situation, by prayer and petition, with thanksgiving, present your requests to God. And the peace of God, which transcends all understanding, will guard your hearts and your minds in Christ Jesus" (Philippians 4:4-7).

Sometimes we need to wait patiently for the answer, but God will always answer:

"Wait for the LORD; be strong, and let your heart take courage; wait for the LORD"" (Psalm 27:14).

"Be still before the LORD and wait patiently for him" (Psalm 37:7).

Look forward to the hope of God's deliverance:

"God is our refuge and strength, an ever-present help in trouble. Therefore we will not fear, though the earth give way and the mountains fall into the heart of the sea" (Psalm 46:1-2).

"Be joyful in hope, patient in affliction, faithful in prayer…" (Romans 12:12).

"…we also rejoice in our sufferings, knowing that suffering produces perseverance; perseverance, character; and character, hope" Romans 5:3-4).

"In all this you greatly rejoice, though now for a little while you may have had to suffer grief in all kinds of trials. These have come so that the proven genuineness of your faith–of greater worth than gold, which perishes even though refined by fire–may result in praise, glory and honor when Jesus Christ is revealed. Though you have not seen Him, you love Him; and even though you do not see Him now, you believe in Him and are filled with an inexpressible and glorious joy, for you are receiving the end result of your faith, the salvation of your souls" (1 Peter 1:6-9).

Jesus tells his disciples in Matthew 6 not to worry or be anxious about the future and reminds them to seek after and focus on the Kingdom that is in the here and now. He tells them, "Therefore do not worry about tomorrow, for tomorrow will worry about itself. Each day has enough trouble of its own (Matthew 6:34)." Daily we are faced with circumstances that can be seen as either a difficulty or an opportunity, it is all a matter of perspective, both of heart and mind. Hope and pessimism cannot coexist.

The choice is ours–will we be a pessimist and allow the difficulties of this world to bring sorrow and discouragement? Or will we be an optimist, recognizing God's sovereignty, and find joy despite the circumstances? Joy begins on our knees. As we are faithful in prayer, confessing, worshiping, and trusting, God is faithful to guide and direct us and bring us through every difficulty, with hope and a joyful heart.

"I will extol the LORD at all times; his
praise will always be on my lips. I will glory
in the LORD; let the afflicted hear and
rejoice. Glorify the LORD with me; let us
exalt his name together. I sought the LORD,
and he answered me; he delivered me from

all my fears…. The righteous cry out, and
the LORD hears them; he delivers them
from all their troubles. The LORD is close
to the brokenhearted and saves those who
are crushed in spirit" (Psalm 34:1-4, 17-18).

Help me not to worry or fret
when things don't go as planned.
Whatever may have caused the fray
help me understand.
What lesson can I learn from this
or what must I confess?
I'll trust you as you guide me
finding joy in your faithfulness.

Six

From Dark Tunnels to Safe Harbors

"I have come into the world as light, so that whoever
believes in me may not remain in darkness"

John 12:46

<u>Dark Tunnels</u>

"The people who walked in darkness have seen a great
light; those who dwelt in a land of deep darkness, on them
has light shone" (Isaiah 9:2).

Do you remember as a child (or maybe a grown-up)
traveling on the road and approaching a tunnel? Someone
yells out, "hold your breath!" There is a huge gasp
followed by a collective silence as everyone in the car tries
to hold their lungs full of air to the other end of the tunnel.
The short tunnels are easy and there is much giggling,
maybe even a sense of accomplishment when we begin to
breathe freely again. But if the tunnel is long and dark, the
longer we try to hold our breath the harder it gets.

I remember feeling lightheaded, panic setting in because I was either going to die of asphyxiation or else feel the shame of not making it to the end of the tunnel. For some, they care nothing about the game, but instead are gripped by fear because to go through a dark tunnel is already suffocating enough; not being able to see what is coming. They are thinking, "Why in the world would I want to hold my breath when even now I feel the walls of the tunnel pressing in on me?"

There are times in our lives when we feel as if we have entered a tunnel. Some are short and we know this. We hold our breath and once we are through, respond with a nervous laugh or a backhand swipe across our brow, and sighing we say, "We made it! We survived that one!" Then there are other times the tunnel is dark and suffocating. We desperately look for the proverbial light at the end of the tunnel, wondering when the darkness and uncertainty will cease. There were times in my life when I had difficulty focusing on the road in front of me rather than the walls pressing in on me.

In my third year in college, I found myself in an especially dark place. Always a good student in the past, now, it seemed, my grades were slipping. I tried to find joy at fraternity parties, drinking, and unhealthy relationships. I had disregarded God, relegating Him to the back roads of my life. This was fun for a while, but as I drove myself further from the truth, the deeper I got into the tunnel, the more miserable and uncomfortable my life became. Having been strong and independent, I didn't want to admit to anyone I was failing, and that my life was spiraling out of control. But God knew. He was merely waiting for me to be ready.

I can still vividly remember the small attic room of the sorority house where I lay on the floor sobbing and begging God to pull me out of the darkness and rescue me from the dark tunnel I had so recklessly driven into. I remember praying, "God, what am I doing to my life? This is not where I want to be going." I asked God to save me from myself and bring people into my life who would encourage me in the right direction. And for the first time in months, I saw daylight! I felt the walls being pushed back and my escape in view.

It was in those desperate moments that God had shown me that He had never abandoned me. I also knew that I still had to travel through the rest of the tunnel. God did not automatically transport me from the darkness in the middle of the tunnel, away from my trial to the open skies with no worries or consequences. No, I still had to learn the lessons, I was still accountable for my choices. Though the light was there waiting for me, I still needed to work on the changes which would have to come into my life and keep moving toward the light. God had taken the blinders off my eyes, and now I needed to keep them open, stay focused and not stall out in the darkness again.

The journey to the end of that place in my life was not easy. Yet when I finally emerged, God did some significant things in my life. He brought a couple of young women to my sorority who were unwavering in their faith and invited me to be a part of a discipleship group specifically geared toward college students. I started attending a local church and Zeta Chi College Fellowship, which became my spiritual boot camp.

God gave me some of my closest and still lifelong friends from that group, and it is where I would eventually meet my future husband! This was also the place where God shored up the foundations of my faith which I had known since I was a child, and I began to finally understand what living with the joy of the Lord meant. "Light dawns in the darkness for the upright; he is gracious, merciful, and righteous" (Psalms 112:4).

Tunnels come in various shapes and sizes. All over the world natural tunnels are carved over time or manmade through remarkable engineering. Most tunnels we encounter have a purpose. They cut through a mountain that would otherwise be impassable, or they cross under a river or even the ocean. Occasionally a tunnel is the only way through the obstacle standing in our path. Yet God is not surprised by the tunnels. He will not abandon us either, because He knows what is on the other side, and we need only to trust Him to guide us through the darkness and into the light. "I am the light of the world. Whoever follows me will not walk in darkness, but will have the light of life" (John 8:12).

However, if we do not remain alert, we may make choices that will take us through dark tunnels when we could have chosen the light. Do not be fooled by the artificial light of wicked men or the temptation to remain in the tunnel. The artificial light, along with the shadows and dark corners, they can all be deceiving. They can make one believe it is safe, even comfortable. The prophet Isaiah cautioned Jerusalem with these words, "Woe to those who call evil good and good evil, who put darkness for light and light for darkness, who put bitter for sweet and sweet for bitter!" (Isaiah 5:20).

"…the path of the righteous is like the light of dawn, which shines brighter and brighter until full day. The way of the wicked is like deep darkness; they do not know over what they stumble." Proverbs 4:18-19

The simple fact that there is sin in the world means that we will all travel through dark tunnels at times. But be aware, some tunnels are created by evil men for the purpose of evil, with hidden passageways for illegal activity, to hide underground what they don't want the world to see. They avoid the light because it exposes their illicit behavior. "And this is the judgement: the light has come into the world, and people loved the darkness rather than the light because their works were evil. For everyone who does wicked things hates the light, lest his works should be exposed. But whoever does what is true comes to the light, so that it may be clearly seen that his works have been carried out in God" (John 3:19-21). Did you know moles not only have poor eyesight, but are also colorblind? The mole's world is a dark, gray, shadowy place. Their entire existence lies within the underground tunnels they create, and because they rarely come into the light, they never see the light the way we do.

"This is the message we have heard from
him and proclaim to you, that God is light,
and in him is no darkness at all.
If we say we have fellowship with him while
we walk in darkness, we lie and do not
practice the truth. But if we walk in the
light, as he is in the light, we have
fellowship with one another, and the blood
of Jesus his Son cleanses us from all sin"
(1 John 1:5-7)

God desires for us to bask in His glorious light, to
not remain in the tunnel of darkness. If we remain in the
darkness too long, we risk losing our vision and ultimately,
our joy. Emerging from the darkness is not easy, especially
if you suffer from anxiety or depression. But God keeps
His promises, and He will not let us be consumed by the
darkness when we search for the light of His steadfast love
and mercy.

"Then they cried to the LORD in their
trouble, and he delivered them from their
distress. He brought them out of darkness
and the shadow of death, and burst their

bonds apart. Let them thank the LORD for

his steadfast love..."

(Psalms 107:13-15a).

And lastly, remember there are times when you may be going through a tunnel to be the light for someone else. By the example of how you walk toward the Light of Christ, you may be saving others from their despair, or drawing them out of their own darkness.

"You are the light of the world...let your light shine before others, so that they may see your good works

and give glory to your Father who is in heaven"

(Matthew 5:14-16).

Bridges

Bridges are a marvelous accomplishment of human engineering and ingenuity. The physics of a suspension bridge is remarkable and incomprehensible to my non-engineering mind. The beauty of those bridges all around the world is each a stunning feat of architecture. However, I find the quaint country bridge has a beauty all its own, reminding me in such simple terms, how Jesus came to be the bridge between our aimless, sinful nature and God's beautiful holiness.

Bridges are usually built because there is something below, which in most cases is uncrossable. To get to the other side, we are required to cross them or find another route. In reaching our destination of heaven, however, Christ as our bridge is the only way to get there. No train ride on the high moral ground or a boat across the river of good deeds will get us there. There is only one bridge that reaches across the divide, Jesus. He paid the toll with His life. When we accept and choose to live life under God's authority, our fees are entirely paid for, and we are free to cross into eternity when our journey on this earth is complete. Jesus said, "I am the way, the truth, and the life. No one comes to the Father except through me" (John 14:6).

As we go through life, we cross many bridges. Some are ordinary little foot bridges taking us from one stage or another, but often they are the milestones in our lives. How many times have we been afraid to cross a bridge or crossed one too hastily? I have a couple of friends who do not like bridges. They avoid them and will take a different route if possible. Occasionally, the sheer height of the bridge causes fear and trepidation. For others, the exceedingly long bridge requires them to trust the soundness of the design across the entire expanse.

Have you faced bridges you didn't want to cross? Responsibilities you weren't sure if you were ready to embrace, such as marriage and children, looking for a new job, or moving to a new city or state. Or maybe you know crossing a particular bridge will be a long and possibly difficult process, for instance going through years of medical school, taking on the responsibility of caring for an elderly parent, or adopting special needs children.

Taking the first step onto the bridge is not easy, crossing to unfamiliar territory, along with its challenges. But refusing to cross the bridge may keep you from experiencing the joy of a new adventure, the joy God has planned for you when He put the bridge in your path. I have had a front-row seat to several families who have chosen to foster and/or adopt children needing a forever home. The process itself is lengthy and arduous, not to mention heartbreaking at times. When they have felt the tug, the call to foster/adopt, often their first reaction is, "Really God, us? Are you sure?" But once they took their first step, they trusted God would bring them to the other side.

Have you ever gone across a wobbly footbridge? I remember as a kid (OK, and maybe even as an adult, too), attempting to run across one of those rickety wooden footbridges. If anyone else jumped on, you better hold on tight! The bridge starts swinging and bouncing and you suddenly feel you are out of control. Do you ever feel as if someone has stepped on your bridge and what you thought would be an easy crossing is unexpectedly not in your control? All you can do is hold on tight.

Trusting God is the only stabilizer when there is no opportunity for turning back. Thus, lean on God to steady the bridge and guide you safely to the other side. Most bridges are crossed without incident, while others will undoubtedly be more treacherous. Yet we all have bridges to cross. They are the transitions in life from one chapter to another. Some are longer than others, some sturdy and firm, while others are like that wobbly footbridge. Just be sure you have chosen wisely the bridges you cross.

Ask for wisdom to know which bridges are yours and be prepared for the kind of bridge you cross. If you know the crossing is going to be a long one, pack plenty of provisions. If you should cross onto the bridge of caring for elderly parents, then gather your resources and a network of support. When my mom was battling Alzheimer's my prayer warriors were extremely important to me. I knew going in the challenge would be difficult, but God gave me a secure safety net and guard rails to get me through to the other side.

Whatever we face in life requires us to seek God's wisdom, particularly when navigating the bridges in our life. "For the LORD gives wisdom; from his mouth come knowledge and understanding; he stores up sound wisdom for the upright; he is a shield to those who walk in integrity, guarding the paths of justice and watching over the way of his saints" (Proverbs 2:6-8).

Safe Harbors

"The LORD is my rock and my fortress and my deliverer, my God, my rock in whom I take refuge" (Psalm 18:2).

One morning I walked under gray skies. The sunlight tried to penetrate through the clouds a few times, but never made an appearance during my walk. I thought about how from time to time our world is under this haze of gloominess, in a fog of despair and uncertainty, desperately trying to find the light of day or a beacon to guide us to safer shores. We get glimpses of the light, and a little bit of hope, then another bank of clouds rolls in, and the fog settles on the edges of the shore making navigation difficult to the harbor's refuge.

At the height of maritime travel and trade, it was the lighthouse—a steadfast, trustworthy, reassuring strength—that brought thousands safely to shore each year. The light steadily emanating from the lantern room meant protection from a rugged shoreline and guidance to safety; this also meant a return to civilization and human presence. Some sought the light because it would bring them salvation and freedom from the oppressive shores they had left behind. And still others were returning to the comfort and familiarity of home.

In difficult or unsettling times, I try to remember these important truths:

There is *always* a beacon of hope, when our hope is in the Lord, because His love and mercies *never* end!

"But this I call to mind, and therefore I have hope: The steadfast love of the LORD never ceases, his mercies never come to an end; they are new every morning; great is your faithfulness. 'The LORD is my portion,' says my soul, 'therefore I will hope in him."

Lamentations 3:21-24

We have a refuge during any storm, and He will bring us through the storm. Not out of it, or around it, but through it, bringing us to a place of refuge, a safe harbor. The storm is still raging, but under God's protection, we can survive. We might still be tossed around, even feeling queasiness in the pit of our stomach, and there may be some damage and repairs to deal with once the storm passes, but we will not be left in the open waters completely alone. Just hold on tight and keep moving toward the light.

"God is our refuge and strength, a very present help in trouble. Therefore we will not fear though the earth gives way, though the mountains be moved into the heart of the sea, though its waters roar and foam, though the mountains tremble at its swelling...Be still and know that I am God...The LORD of hosts is with us; the God of Jacob is our fortress." (Psalm 46:1-3,10,11).

Isn't this a comfort knowing God is right there with us during the storm? Sometimes we simply need to be still and stand within the fortress, allowing His presence to hold us, guide us, and bring us through the storm. Jesus is our lighthouse in a dark world. If we keep our eyes on him and focus on the light instead of the raging sea around us or the jagged rocks hidden in the fog, we can get through to safe harbors. However, I don't want to be like Peter. Even though he did as God asked him and walked out onto the water, he lost sight of Jesus.

When Peter decided to focus on the circumstances, he became frightened and began to sink. Yet, Jesus never lost sight of him, and as Peter cried out for help, Jesus reached out and took hold of him. Jesus asked him, "O you of little faith, why did you doubt?" When we have that abiding faith and trust, we can step out onto the waters, and walk to the One who will hold us up and bring us to safety. Doubting or losing hope can be easy when we are caught in the storm, but Jesus wants to be our place of confidence and hope.

Most of us do not plan for a journey buffeted by storms. Yet, we may unexpectedly find the shoreline more rugged and the safe harbor more difficult to find. Trying to navigate the crazy storms of this life can be challenging for any of us. I have spent far too much time focusing on the circumstances rather than on the steady Light of hope. But, when I began emerging from the fog, my heart found joy again, and God restored my hope. Do not lose heart. God's light will break through the darkness, He is our refuge, our beacon of hope, and our strength. God is faithful.

"Light is sown for the righteous, and joy for the upright in heart. Rejoice in the LORD, O you righteous, give thanks to his holy name!" (Psalms 97:11-12).

Whatever obstacles we face, we can keep traveling forward with God's strength. Whether you find yourself in the midst of a dark tunnel, traversing a long or shaky bridge, or caught in a stormy season of life, God does not intend for you to go it alone. He will provide for you His wisdom, the strength and support of others, and a way of escape if necessary.

"The LORD is a stronghold for the oppressed, a stronghold in times of trouble. And those who know your name put their trust in you, for you, O LORD, have not forsaken those who seek you" (Psalm 9:9-10).

Life can take me through tunnels at times
Where shadows and darkness reside in my mind.
Yet when I can keep God's Word in my sight
He helps me walk out of darkness, into the Light
The bridges that I face at times
Some are hard and some are kind.
But when I cross, I can be sure
By seeking your wisdom, I am secure.
Though storms may toss me into distress
I can fully depend on my rock and fortress.
You are my refuge at the edge of the shore
My trustworthy, steadfast, and safe harbor.

Seven

Steppingstones or Stumbling Blocks?

"I have taught you the way of wisdom; I have led you in
the paths of uprightness. When you walk, your step will not
be hampered, and if you run, you will not stumble"

Proverbs 4:11-12

When you look at the path before you, do you see
steppingstones or stumbling blocks? As a kid, I loved
finding a way to cross the creek on the steppingstones
barely emerging above the surface of the water. While
others were cautious, I saw it as a challenge to be
conquered. And although my goal may have been to get to
the other side, with each step I focused on choosing the
stone which would hold and carry me to the next step. One
miscalculation and I would find myself on my backside
soaking wet as the waters of the little creek were forced to
meander around my unfortunate disruption to its peaceful
existence.

Why did I fall? Maybe because the stone was slippery and slimy from a gentle covering of moss, or even though the stone appeared solid, the lack of a secure foundation underneath made it wobble, and to my dismay, there was no hope of avoiding the awkward tumble. At that moment, I had to decide if I would let the plunge into the creek discourage me or fill me with the determination to keep going in the face of adversity.

Now, mind you, falling into a creek a few inches deep would usually be considered a minor inconvenience; yet how we handle little adversities or manage the small steppingstones in our lives are the lessons God uses to prepare us for the boulders and sometimes the mountains we may have to climb over to get to the other side. Can you rejoice even when the steppingstones are not as secure as you thought?

Navigating the Stumbling Stones

What kind of adversities do you face? Much needed car repairs, a broken air conditioner in 90-degree temperatures, or a disobedient toddler? What about an unreasonable supervisor, financial difficulty, or a cancer diagnosis? Some may seem small in comparison to others, but the degree of difficulty can often be measured by the way in which we respond to the challenge. A few years ago, we were on our way back from an Angels Baseball road trip in Arizona. We were on the home stretch. It was late. We were hungry. We stopped for something to eat in Palm Desert and as we got up to leave, I left my phone on the table.

I realized this as we were getting into the car and quickly went back in to retrieve it. Unfortunately, in those few moments, someone had decided they would take my phone and keep it for themselves. We tried to locate it but to no avail. I was overcome by an avalanche of emotions...sad, angry (at both myself and the perpetrator), violated, and disappointed just to name a few. Yet my dear husband patiently waited for me to calm down and reminded me it was only a phone that could be replaced, and it wasn't the end of the world! It was, however, the end of the pictures I had taken on the trip, but still, nothing to cry over.

You know the expression, *don't cry over spilt milk?* Why do we say that? Because once the milk is spilt, there is no way of putting it all back into the glass. What's done is done. You can't change the fact the milk spilled, so we clean it up and move on. The way in which we handle the inconvenience of the spilt milk, from our attitude to our response, is often an indication of how we will respond to the greater adversities we face.

What happens when the "spilt milk" gets into the crevices of our lives, when maybe that small glass of milk is the only one you would get for months and now is gone? This is when it is no longer an inconvenience, but a greater challenge that we are faced with. Losing a phone is one thing, but what if you are facing something much greater, such as a cancer diagnosis? Our pastor's wife, Susie, has been facing this for over four years.

Susie was diagnosed with stage 4 colon cancer in 2019. It soon spread to her liver. She has dealt with chemo, radiation, numerous procedures and surgeries, and the rollercoaster ride of good days and bad days, great days, and absolutely awful days. Yet, through all of it, many of us are inspired by her joyful spirit and her attitude in the midst of the difficult road before her. I sat down with her one afternoon and asked her how she remains joyful despite the circumstances.

_Me:_ How would you describe joy?

Susie: Peace and contentment. And enjoyment no matter what is going on and happening to you.

Me: Have you always had an attitude of joy? If not, what changed?

Susie: I was not a very joyful child and teenager. I was negative and had to work hard at smiling. That would sometimes make me feel better. As a young adult I found I had to work at being joyful, but in the last ten years or so I finally felt as if joy came more naturally. I found joy in both the simple and hard part of life. What changed? Spending time in God's Word. Learning and knowing God says we will have tribulation and the righteous will be tested. I fought so hard to have 'the good life', then God revealed to me we need to let go of that longing and realize 'the good life' will only come when we are in heaven.

Me: When life gets really hard, what is the source of your joy?

Susie: Solely relying on God's love, trusting He is going to walk with me no matter how hard it gets, and knowing His will is perfect. I go to the Psalms a lot."

Me: How does your faith have an impact on your joy, or the lack of?

Susie: Faith has a huge impact, because when my faith wasn't strong and things didn't happen how I wanted them to, I got angry. I thought, 'What did I do wrong?' Now I trust the outcome even when I don't understand it. There is a reason for it.

Me: After God, who do you seek counsel and advice from? What part does community have in experiencing joy?

Susie: My husband, Ron. We can talk it out loud with each other and work it through. My children as they are getting older (teenagers) have wise things to teach me. There are women in our church I can be vulnerable with, which is unusual for a pastor's wife, but I have a whole community of women I can go to.

Me: Is there an internal struggle when putting on a brave and joyful front?

Susie: I don't feel like I have to be or do anything different because I am a pastor's wife. Some days I know I need extra strength because I just honestly don't feel like being joyful. However, I do feel like I have the freedom to say when I am having a bad day. David is a good example of crying out and being vulnerable before God.

Me: How has the cancer affected your joy?

Susie: At the very beginning we ran to God, became more fervent in reading scripture, praying, and wrestling with it, of course. We trusted God's will. Ministry life looks different now, and I have had to trust Him when having to say no to ministry I loved doing before my cancer.

I created blessing stones, drawing stone walls in my journal, and keeping a record of God's blessings by writing them inside the stones. They are my ebenezer stones.

As a result, I had a joyful and positive attitude. Then the more I added stones, the easier it became to have a joyful attitude. Now I look at walking through difficulties with a trust in God even if I don't understand. Yes, it may still be difficult, but God is sovereign! My attitude has a positive effect on my family. We rely on humor a lot! I have actually experienced a different level of joy because of my cancer. I was grumpy and pushing through life, but not now. I am definitely more joyful than before.

Cancer was not a path Susie would have chosen, but it was one of the stones God placed before her. She and her family could have seen the cancer as a stumbling block of dreams destroyed and future expectations dashed. She could have lived in misery because of the physical and emotional loss and pain. But because Susie has put complete faith and trust in the One who laid the stones, she knew her Father in heaven would walk with her every step of the way and make even the most difficult steps passable. God has been faithful to Susie and her family through every trial, great and small, why would this time be any different?

Her journey is a beautiful example of what it means to "consider it all joy when facing trials of various kinds"[6].

Christ as the Cornerstone and Laying a Firm Foundation

Consider when you walk on a path of steppingstones and pavers in a lovely garden. The designer of the garden curated the path and calculated how many stones he would need and how they would be placed along the path. He took care to place them evenly and strategically so those who walked the path would not stumble. However, over time, the ground has settled, and the erosion from storms and maybe a bit of overgrowth has caused the stones to become uneven.

God has designed a path for us and set out steppingstones for us to follow, but the results of sin and a fallen world will at times make our paths difficult. The original stones are still there, but do we look at them as stumbling blocks, or do we trust God will hold our hand, even carry us over the damaged path and bring us back to level ground? The thing about God's steppingstones is they are always secure. When we step onto the path He has laid out before us, we can be assured it is the best path, the one

[6] James 1:2.

111

which brings more joy than sorrow. Does that mean the path is easy? Not necessarily, in fact, usually not.

A carefully marked path with steppingstones and a clear trail is easy if we are paying attention. A highway that is well-lit and that has frequent road signs makes the navigation of a trip much easier. But not every road or path is marked clearly. Some are even hidden or laden with obstacles. The path is still there, and the road is still on the map, but we may have to work harder, go slower, or study the map longer to reach our destination without disaster.

A stumbling stone as described in the Old and New Testament uses the Hebrew word *mikšól*, which is similar to a snare or trap, and the Greek word *Proskomma* which refers to a type of barrier. Both are tools of Satan. One will set a snare or temptation. If we fall for it, we may leave the path God has laid out for us and go another way. Or Satan will throw up a barrier, to either keep us from moving forward, or even convince us to retreat, turn back, and give up. He may even put out counterfeit stones which appear solid but are unreliable and broken.

God, however, has set before us steppingstones of mercy and grace, of hope and endurance. This is because He set Jesus as the cornerstone, the firm foundation in which we can put our trust. 1 Peter 2:4 tells us Jesus is the "living stone" bringing life to those who believe in him, but to those who do not, those who reject Him as the only foundation for a joyful and abundant life, will stumble.

Behold I am laying in Zion a stone, a cornerstone chosen
and precious, and whoever believes in him
will not be put to shame.' So the honor is for you who
believe, but for those who do not believe, "The stone that
the builders rejected has become the cornerstone' and 'A
stone of stumbling, and rock of offense.' They stumble
because they disobey the word." (1Peter 2:6-8)

Each day when you step out onto the path, rejoice that Jesus is your foundation and He will hold you up even if the road gets rough in places. David had a profound joy in the LORD, and he especially rejoiced in God's law and His many precepts. He made it abundantly clear how important it was to know God's Word, meditate on it, and live by His commandments. He said this is the result, "I rejoice at your word like one who finds great spoil...Great peace have those who love your law; nothing can make them stumble." Psalm 119:162, 165. Abide in God and in His laws, trust and rejoice in Him and He will keep you from stumbling.

The One Who Guides Our Path

On a recent women's retreat, I took an early morning hike on one of the camp trails. At times a path is made harder by obstacles, but sometimes they are affected by our own limitations. I was once very athletic, but time and age, added weight and knee replacement surgery have put limitations on my body even though my mind still wants to do challenging things. So, did my limitations stop me from climbing the mountain? They could have, but I chose to work within my limitations because I knew if I reached my goal, there would be a beautiful reward at the top.

The hike was relatively easy at first. I occasionally stopped to take pictures which broke up the climb. Patches of fog hung in the air on that crisp and chilly spring morning. Sunlight filtered through the towering trees and a slight breeze gently drifted through the leaves of their branches. I could hear them almost whisper to me, encouraging me to the top of each little hill. God's beautiful creation surrounded me, and it was exhilarating.

I could clearly see the dirt path even with the scattered leaves and occasional stone, or unearthed root to navigate around. Once the incline became a little steeper, my breathing became more labored and my heart began to beat faster. Just as my legs began to feel the heaviness of each step, there in front of me were wooden planks embedded in the path to make it more stable. Then the path grew tougher, and I had to push myself or turn around and go back. So, God and I had a little conversation. I asked Him for the strength to make it to the top, to keep from falling, and to trust the path laid out before me.

As I reached the top of the steps, I knew my goal was only a short way further around the bend and up the hill. On this part of the path the blanket of leaves was thicker. They crunched under my feet, causing my foot to slip here and there. I finally pushed through a stand of bushes and there it was–the top of the hill! The sight was glorious. A view of the tree-filled valley, laden with fog, lie before me. A ridge of mountains stood in the distance, and moments before the sun made its appearance, various hues of pink and golden clouds hung in the sky.

In the foreground of a dirt clearing framed with trees and boulders, there stood an empty cross. I was in awe of the beauty and the stillness as peace and joy washed over me. I had made this hike before. This time, however, the path was harder than I had remembered, but the reward was almost sweeter because God used the path to teach me lessons about my character and spoke to my heart about decisions I was struggling with. That path, with all its quiet, peaceful places, also had hard places and challenges. The path had a purpose. It took me to my destination and taught me in ways a simple walk down the road may not have.

God will use every path and every road we take to teach us something. Are we willing to step out on each path, trusting He will walk with us through the obstacles or uneven steppingstones? And while we are taking the path, will we find joy in what we see and hear and learn? Over the years a verse that has been reassuring to me is "The steps of a man are established by the LORD, and he delights in his way; when he falls, he will not be hurled headlong, because the LORD is the One who holds his hand" (Psalm 37:23-24, NASB1995).

Offering a Hand and Clearing the Way

There are also times when we are given opportunities to help one another when the path gets tangled, or the road gets rough. Have you ever gone on a hike where the trail was uneven, where maybe a tree or rocks have fallen across the trail? It is much easier to overcome those obstacles when hiking buddies help each other navigate the challenge, someone who will take your hand or who lends a shoulder as you cross the log blocking your way. It is the same with the obstacles in our lives. Trials are much easier to face when friends and family come alongside, and not so impossible to "consider it all joy" when we face various trials. The key is knowing who your traveling buddies are and they are only a phone call or text away from lending the support you need to navigate the obstacles when they appear.

Not only do we need the occasional boost, but we can also make ourselves available to those around us who may need a hand over their own log. Just as fellow hikers should be alert and attentive when walking a trail, being observant of each other's safety, we too can be attentive when someone in our life is in distress, when the path they are on is blocked or hindered. Those traveling companions have an important role in how we navigate the rough patches in our lives and whether we consider them adventures rather than hinderances.

Remember, knowing we are on the right path means we can rejoice even when God uses the most challenging of circumstances for our good and His glory. For this reason, it is tremendously important to be in community with other believers to "encourage one another and build one another up" (1 Thessalonians 5:11). Practically speaking, when a family must pack up their home and move, can you spare a couple of hours to pack boxes or watch the kids so mom and dad can pack? If a friend needs a ride to the doctor or is recovering from surgery and needs their house cleaned, are you there?

When I was recovering from my knee replacement surgery, the community of family and friends who came alongside me and my husband was truly a blessing. Not only did they provide meals and encouragement, but one of my sweet friends even helped me wash my hair! The road to recovery can often be scattered with obstacles, but I was able to remain encouraged and mostly joyful because of the support and prayers from my family and friends. And of course, God's hand was there and held me up all along the way!

Some roads have yet to be traveled and are waiting to be paved. God may require some of us to do the work of removing the debris and making the path clear, to pave the way for those who follow. The pioneers who traveled across the great plains to the West Coast of the United States in the early 1800s, traveled where there were no roads and cleared the way as they went. They forged ahead into the unknown, some for adventure, others for fame or fortune, many sought a better life, and some went out as missionaries.

You can read the biographies of almost any of the early missionaries and quickly realize they had not chosen the easy path. Many traveled to villages and territories that had never heard the Gospel before. They learned and translated the Bible into their own language, sometimes creating a written language from scratch. They faced many hardships, difficult living conditions, days or months of arduous travel, hunger, sickness, and in some cases death.

God had called them to pave the way for the Gospel and for others to follow the paths they had cleared so churches could be built, and lives could be transformed through the power of the Gospel. Today's missionaries still face some of these challenges, along with cultural barriers, prejudice, and countries ravaged by war and oppression. Their journeys are hard. Oh, but the joy they have in seeing lives changed and hearts coming to Christ!

If you are not called to be a missionary, you still may be called to forge the way for a new ministry, join a new project at work, or reach out to a new community where you have recently moved. All may require moving a few stones, clearing the path. It could be bumpy at first, but even in this, God desires for us to take on the challenge with the joy of knowing we are serving Him.

At other times, we are the ones waiting until the road is cleared. Waiting is hard but may be necessary to pass through safely. Have you ever sat through a weather delay at the airport? Recently, we were caught in a four-hour rain delay in Sacramento, California on our way home from my niece's wedding. It was inconvenient and created some stress, nonetheless, we had no choice but to wait it out and make the best of it. With interest, I observed how some of our fellow travelers handled the delay. Some complained on their phone to friends or family members, while others ate a meal, took a nap, or passed the time on their phone or computer. One person paced and continually asked an attendant about our flight status.

The people I enjoyed watching the most were the families who played games together to pass the time, or those having enjoyable conversations between friends and acquaintances. How we wait and the attitude we display not only affects our own level of joy but can have a positive or negative impact on those around us. How does God want us to wait? What storm in life are you waiting on until it passes through? A job search or infertility. Grief at the loss of a loved one or a prodigal child. A soldier at war or a chronic illness.

Noah waited for the waters to recede before releasing his passengers who were undoubtedly looking forward to standing on dry ground. Abraham waited for the promised blessing of a son at an unlikely age. Hannah also waited for a much-desired child. Job waited for God to relieve him of his misery and Joseph waited to be released from prison. The Israelites waited for their freedom from slavery, then waited 40 more years for a permanent home in the promised land. David waited to be king while a fugitive. The Jews waited 80 years to return from exile, then waited over 400 years for the Messiah. Jesus waited 30 years to begin his ministry, and Paul waited in prison for the chance to share the Gospel with the emperor of Rome.

That is a lot of waiting. Most of these waited graciously and trusted God for the results. There are also those who did not wait with the proper attitude or acceptance of God's plan, and many paid dearly for it. Some chose their own path or tried to hurry God along such as Eli's disobedient sons, Hophni and Phinehas, King Saul's impatience with God, Absalom's rebellion, Rehoboam's heavy-handedness, Jonah fleeing God's command, and the greed of Ananias and Sapphira.

I love David's heart in Psalm 27. The first verse says, "The LORD is my light and my salvation; whom shall I fear? The LORD is the stronghold of my life; of whom shall I be afraid?" And the last verse says, "Wait for the LORD; be strong, and let your heart take courage; wait for the LORD!" In between, David acknowledges he is facing huge adversaries, yet he remains confident and keeps his eyes on "the beauty of the LORD." He knows God will give him shelter and he rejoices that the LORD will answer him when he cries for help. David asks God to teach him and lead him, then looks expectantly upon the LORD…and waits.

Whatever the steps laid for us on our journey, we can trust a faithful God who will be right there with us. He will either clear the path or hold our hand and walk us through each difficulty and trial. But He will never leave us without the encouragement, endurance, and support needed to face even the most difficult trial. And each stone on the way has a purpose, whether it is simply to keep us on the right path, or to test and strengthen our faith, producing steadfastness and the full effect of being perfect and complete, lacking in nothing. When you look at the path before you do you see stumbling blocks or steppingstones? It is all a matter of perspective.

Along the path are steppingstones
to guide me through the day
Although sometimes I stumble
if I choose a slippery way.
As I navigate the stumbling stones
that might be at my feet
Help me see the road more clearly,
so I do not find defeat.
May I be a strength for those
who need a helping hand
And offer ways to pull them up
so on their feet they'll land.
I know I won't be cast headlong
or fall upon my face
For you've put me on firm footing
of your steadfast love and grace.

Eight

"Are we there yet?"
Anticipation and Hope

"I wait for the LORD, my soul waits,
and in his word I hope"
Psalm 130:5

When we talked about the destination in Chapter 2, I referred to the importance of setting goals and knowing where you are going. Once the goal is set, and the plan is put into motion, we usually look forward to reaching that goal with great anticipation. This would be like the carload of children filled with excitement as they drive ever closer to the amusement park; the engaged couple enthusiastically planning their upcoming wedding; or the college student who looks expectantly to future possibilities as graduation draws near. These are but a few of the many things in life we look forward to, especially when we step closer to our desired goal. Our hopes and dreams are what motivate us to keep going.

We also discussed how the roadblocks and detours could completely change the landscape of our plans. Moving forward becomes a monumental task if those plans are delayed or dashed, even causing heartbreak when they do not come to fruition. Depending on our perspective, the waiting, the longing for something which is beyond the horizon can be exciting and motivating, or the opposite, it can be disheartening and hopeless.

How do we live with joy in whatever our current circumstances may be?
By remembering joy and hope go hand in hand.

I freely admit joy is hard to find when we are surrounded by fear, oppression, sickness, or sorrow. I am convinced true joy is fleeting if there is an absence of hope. Unfortunately, many times we are offered a counterfeit hope... hope of success, hope for wealth, hope in government, to name a few. Each of these are a false hope, a temporary hope, which does not remain and eventually brings disappointment. However, an eternal hope, the hope God promises when we put our trust in him, will never disappoint. And it is this eternal hope which gives us cause for joy, for whatever we face on our earthly journey pales in comparison to what waits for us at our final destination, heaven.

"Hope deferred makes the heart sick, but a
desire fulfilled is a tree of life"
(Proverbs 13:12).

I have witnessed the sorrow and anger of a person who has no active faith in God. When they experience the loss of a loved one, or property or wealth, they are often driven to despair, in a vicious cycle of hopelessness. Yet, when these calamities fall on the path of a Christian, one who has a clear understanding of God's sovereignty, there is an abiding hope, a trust that God will comfort, restore, provide, and strengthen those whose faith is not in worldly promises, but instead genuine hope.

Not a hope that God will fix everything and make it better, but the hope of knowing He will provide the endurance and perseverance to run the race to reach the finish line, and the eternal reward will be well worth the training, sacrifice, and challenges along the way. Is there still disappointment, grief, and pain? Yes, of course. God does not want us to be void of emotion, but He does not want our emotions to take us over either. Emotions are what give us empathy and compassion for what others are going through. But if we remain with fear and anxiety, anger and pride, sorrow, and regret, we may become stalled in self-centered emotions.

Consequently, we must not camp there, but instead allow peace to cast out fear, patience to override anger, and joy to mingle with sorrow. The fruit of the Spirit - love, joy, peace, patience, kindness, goodness, faithfulness, gentleness, and self-control[7] are others-focused emotions and actions. They draw us away from self-centered despair, hostility, or bitterness, toward a heart full of hope. Hope moves us forward onto the well-lit road, despair pulls back into the dark, shadowy alleys. Do not despair, have hope, and walk in the Light.

The Road to Nowhere

There is a road in Alaska called the Road to Nowhere. It is on the Gravina Islands of the Alexander Archipelago in southeastern Alaska. The road was built to connect the island to a highway going to Ketchikan but was never completed. There is nothing at the end. It truly goes

---

[7] Galatians 5:22-23.

nowhere. At times we may feel we are also going nowhere, or like we have reached the end of the road. We keep looking off into the distance, hoping to reach something, anything but the same landscape over and over again. Spinning your wheels and going nowhere definitely has a chilling effect on our ability to have hope. But God does not desire us to be stuck in a rut, going nowhere. If you are sensing your life has no direction and no end goal, the time may have come to reevaluate.

Are you struggling with a habitual sin such as anger, lying, overspending, pornography, or maybe excessive drinking? You try repeatedly to overcome, but each time you fail, the hopelessness sinks deeper into your heart. But God is the God of hope, of redemption, who can and will place you on a road leading to beautiful places of grace and forgiveness. Satan will try and deceive you, fill your heart with self-doubt, and tell you that you are a failure. But he lies! We are sinners, yes. We will make mistakes and bad choices, yes. Sometimes more than once…or twice…you know what I mean. But we are redeemed by the Blood of the Lamb, and God does not keep an account of wrongs. Do not allow Satan to deceive you and shout accusations at you. Throw up your shield of Faith and extinguish his fiery darts.

God's plan will never put us on a road to nowhere. Remember, we were created to bring God glory and to enjoy Him forever! Again, if you feel you are on a road to nowhere, examine how and why you got there. Go before the throne of grace and lay at His feet all your hopelessness, acknowledging if there is any sin, and confess those sins, confess your fears, your anxiety, your helplessness.

Are you a perfectionist? Do you feel the need to grasp the steering wheel tighter and be in control of everything, and when you're not, do you consider yourself a failure? Then do this: put out your hands. Clinch them tightly and think of all the things you are holding onto which are not healthy, all the things pulling you down a dead-end street. Now, open your hands, palms up, and let go. Surrender all of it, give everything to Jesus. Not merely as a symbolic gesture, but truly surrender everything in your heart.

Talk to Jesus and say a prayer something like this: *Jesus, I confess that I am hopeless and lost. I confess that even though I have surrendered my life to you, I am still holding on to pieces of it for my own fleshly pleasures or because I foolishly believe I need to do this one thing by myself without your help. Forgive me, Jesus. Lord Jesus,*

give me the strength and the courage to let go and to
completely surrender to your will. I admit what I am going
through right now cannot be overcome by my own strength,
but only by the power of your Holy Spirit correcting me,
teaching me, guiding me, and holding me up. Lord, restore
my hope, give me wisdom, and help me know the joy of the
Lord. You are a good, good Father and I give you all the
praise and the glory.

Rejoice in Hope

What in your life are you waiting for? For your
unbelieving family member or friend to come to Jesus'
saving grace? For God to release you from the pain of
infertility and bring you the long-prayed-for child? What
road to nowhere are you traveling on? A joyless job with
no hope of advancement? A never-ending cycle of debt and
living paycheck to paycheck? God does not want any of us
to live a life of despair and hopelessness, but a life filled
with joy and the hope of the Lord. The first step is an
attitude of the heart, which is usually the hardest. To put
our complete trust in God's intended outcome and not ours
should not be scary but freeing. When the circumstances
around you seem bleak, don't hold on tighter but surrender
the situation completely to Him.

If you find yourself on your knees crying out to God with your confession, your praise, and your request, He will hear you. Then ask, "God what do you want me to do? What do you want me to release, and what do you want me to take hold of?" Ask for wisdom about what can and needs to be done to either change or accept the circumstances. Ask God if there is a reason you are in that miserable job. For instance, is there someone who will only hear about Jesus if you are working there? Or is there someone who needs your comfort and encouragement?

If change is the desired outcome, then with His wisdom and discernment seek the help you need to bring about change. Does your situation require medical attention, the counsel of a pastor or mentor, a financial advisor, or a job counselor? How about a friend who helps you get out of bed in the morning? The adage, misery loves company, is only true if misery is what you're choosing. But if you desire a life of hope and joy, surround yourself with individuals and a community of believers who cultivate and nurture hope and joy, who run to hope, not away from it.

For most of us, life is a series of marathons. We can start out strong, exhilarated by the adventure and the newness of the race. But as the miles build up so does the weariness, sometimes pain, and brokenness. The runner's breathing becomes harder and more labored, just as a difficult situation in our life may bring suffocating sadness, anxiety, worry, or anger. Here is where all the training and preparation comes into play, looking deep within for the inner strength to press on past what runners call, the wall. Trusting God means calling on the Holy Spirit to give us the strength to press on.

Sometimes pressing forward is hard, isn't it? How do we go forward when the finish line is seemingly beyond our reach or maybe even feels like it keeps changing? Paul says, "But one thing I do: forgetting what lies behind and straining forward to the goal for the prize of the upward call of God in Christ Jesus" (Philippians 3:13-15). When we remember the goal, the finish line, we can press on even when it is hard, even when we don't feel like it. Pressing forward is not passive, but active, therefore we should be asking God, *what do you want me to do right now, how do I keep pressing forward and how can I make a difference for Your Kingdom?*

That final push often comes from the community we surround ourselves with. In a marathon, there is greater motivation to keep going when we have the support of family and friends cheering us on and providing encouragement with physical and emotional support. A well-organized race has event personnel who provide water and nourishment, medical staff if a runner is in distress or injured, and volunteers who keep the road clear of obstacles and the runners on the right path. Do you have that kind of support in your own life? Who are your cheerleaders? Who is on your support team? The way God tangibly gives you strength is most often through the support and strength of others. Consequently, if you struggle with having hope in whatever you are facing, assemble a team who can walk alongside you, and when needed, can carry you to the finish line.

At the beginning of the isolation of 2020, I was determined to not let fear or isolation steal my joy for life. But as the days wore on, it was not easy to stay true to my determination of being joyful during a pandemic. There were days when I drifted into despair, the loneliness and mundane routine closing in on me. With each new setback, the hope of returning to normal seemed bleak and distant. But then I was reminded of a few basic truths; God is sovereign; God has equipped the church and every Christian to persevere in the face of persecution and trials. This is not our home, we are not of this world, but we are God's chosen people, redeemed for a purpose. Our contentment does not depend on our circumstances, but on the attitude of our hearts. We are to be at peace with all men, for the battle belongs to the Lord. Lastly, we have an eternal hope when this marathon is over, our great reward will be no more sorrow, no more pain, and an eternity with the King of the Universe.

In the last few chapters, there has been a lot of focus on all the roadblocks and detours, whether they be obstacles or merely unexpected changes in the landscape. We have established that we will face trials of various kinds and the road we walk on is often marked with suffering. May we not forget, however, that there is always hope, and that knowing and understanding hope comes from being in God's Word every day. Paul wrote this to the Romans, "For whatever was written in former days was written for our instruction, that through endurance and through the encouragement of the Scriptures we might have hope" (Romans 15:4). As practical examples, there are a few steps I take to maintain a good dose of hope and joy in my life, and when necessary, to pull me out of a discouraging day or situation.

First, I have collected a list of verses I keep at the ready in my phone or Bible. I meditate on them and pray through them. I love to pray scripture, using my name or someone I am praying for, and applying it to the current situation. I also love music, and I have a playlist filled with songs of encouragement and hope, praises to God, and songs that motivate me and give me a kick in the pants. Every time I hear a song with a great message, it is added to my playlist. And artists that sing scripture are definitely a bonus!

Finally, I have prayer warriors whom I know I can go to, even if it is a simple text to pray for me with little or no explanation. Prayer, God's Word, accountability, and a fellowship of believers are what keep me sane, hopeful, and joyful when the rest of the world is chaotic and hopeless.

Therefore, here are verses we can meditate on to remind us even when the road is hard, hope and joy must remain:

Acts 2:25-28 (Psalm 16:8-11) - I saw the LORD always before me; for he is at my right hand that I may not be shaken. Therefore my heart is glad, and my whole being rejoices; my flesh also will dwell in hope. For you will not abandon my soul to Hades, or let your holy one see corruption. You make known to me the path of life; in your presence there is fullness of joy.

Psalm 71:1-5, 14 - In you, O LORD, do I take refuge; let me never be put to shame! In your righteousness deliver me and rescue me; incline your ear to me, and save me! Be to me a rock of refuge, to which I may continually come; you have given the command to save me, for you are my rock and my fortress. Rescue me, O my God, from the hand of the wicked, from the grasp of the unjust and cruel man. For you, O Lord, are my hope, my trust, O LORD, from my youth...But I will hope continually and will praise you yet more and more.

Psalm 119:114 - You are my hiding place and my shield; I hope in your word.

Psalm 147:11 - but the LORD takes pleasure in those who fear him, in those who hope in his steadfast love.

Proverbs10:28 - The hope of the righteous brings joy, but the expectations of the wicked will perish.

Lamentations 3:21-24 - But this I call to mind, and therefore I have hope: The steadfast love of the LORD never ceases; his mercies never come to an end; they are new every morning; great is your faithfulness. "The LORD is my portion," says my soul, "therefore I will hope in him."

Romans 12:12 - Rejoice in hope, be patient in tribulation, be constant in prayer.

Romans 15:13 - May the God of hope fill you with all joy and peace in believing, so that by the power of the Holy Spirit you may abound in hope.

Why is it hard to be patient and wait
to achieve all that we anticipate.
Or when the road goes nowhere, it seems,
as my hopes are dashed and so too my dreams.
That's when my hope must be in You
to find the strength to see it through.
To surrender all in Jesus' name
where hope and joy will still remain

Nine

Traveling Companions

"Whoever walks with the wise becomes wise,
but the companion of fools will suffer harm"
Proverbs 13:20

Have you ever traveled with grumpy children, whether they be yours or someone else's? The incessant complaining and whining can weigh on you by the end of the trip. In fact, before we know it, we can be sucked into doing the very thing we detest, complaining about the complainers! When we are in the presence of complainers, they can influence us into joining the chorus of moans and groans, and snippy comments; or we can choose to do our part to change the atmosphere of discontent by redirecting the complaints into "only what is helpful for building others up"[8].

---

[8] Ephesians 3:29.

One of our four children let us know in the first couple years of his little life that he did not like the car seat in any way, shape, or form! This made road trips quite challenging for our family, especially our trip across the country. Now, we couldn't just leave him home or ship him on ahead, tempting as that might have been, so we devised creative ways to keep him occupied and as happy as possible. And, of course, I am grateful we made the effort to find a way, because there were far more delightful moments than discontented ones, from our otherwise happy little guy. Discontentment can breed more discontentment unless we make a conscious effort to be satisfied with our circumstances rather than miserable.

Are we careful not to be the cause of someone else's misery because of our own grumbling and complaining? We may very well become the catalyst for stealing their joy. In my lifetime I have been guilty of grumbling and whining far more than I care to admit. I have been known to be opinionated and outspoken on occasion. Sometimes I say out loud what should stay in my head, or never be there in the first place. I really didn't want to be 'the one' spoiling everyone's trip because of my discontentment.

For years, it rarely occurred to me that my "honest opinion" was grumbling and complaining. When I was called out for doing so, I had to work at changing the attitude of my heart. My desire was to create fun, laughter, and joyful memories for our kids. I wanted to travel with happy campers, too! A dissatisfied or grumpy attitude of the heart can spoil all the joy, and over time I have become better at sowing seeds of contentment rather than the seeds of discontentment.

There are times when sending the grumblers on their way is needed and seeking out traveling companions with joyful, encouraging attitudes is the better choice. When we first begin our journey through life, we are given traveling companions such as parents or grandparents, siblings, or teachers. Ones we are expected to learn how to get along with. When there is conflict, however, the road traveled with them is bumpy, uncomfortable, and at times even scary or dangerous. Once we are older, our traveling companions are more determined by our own choices. Some will become lifelong companions, such as our spouse, dear friends, mentors, and counselors. Others are acquaintances, such as co-workers, teammates, and classmates.

The people that we choose to travel through life with can have an immense effect on how joyful or miserable the journey will be. We must choose wisely and carefully when developing our closest relationships. They will become some of our greatest influencers; whether that is for good or evil may depend upon the ones we choose. There may be times, however, when the companions we have taken become a negative influence on our life. They may lead us down dark and unhealthy paths, damaging our witness and sullying our character. They may throw up roadblocks, discouraging us and holding us back, instead of building us up and helping us grow. Worst of all, they may vandalize the relationship by being verbally or physically abusive. In these circumstances, it may be necessary for you to part ways with someone who hinders your journey and steals your joy.

I am primarily referring to relationships not bound by marriage, parent/child, or siblings. When at all possible, these relationships need to be honored, and when necessary, healed and restored. I do understand, however, there may be biblical grounds to bring some relationships to an end when extreme or irreconcilable circumstances exist. In those situations, seek trusted, godly counsel and protection if necessary. Maintaining positive, healthy

141

relationships can be challenging in our current culture, even under the best of circumstances. Therefore, we should carefully choose with whom we surround ourselves when traveling through this lifelong journey.

When God sent Abram to a land far from his family, He did not send him alone. He traveled with his wife, Sarai, and his nephew Lot, along with an entire host of servants[9]. Later, Lot became a hindrance to Abram's journey, and they parted ways.

God did not send Moses to face Pharaoh alone. He gave him his brother Aaron to support and encourage him. Theirs was not a perfect relationship and Aaron later failed him miserably in the desert. Eventually, Joshua became Moses' closest companion instead. Jonathan was David's dearest friend, who proved to be pivotal in saving both David's life and his future reign as king. David's trusted relationship with the Prophet Nathan proved valuable in his correction and repentance when he strayed from God's plan.

Rehoboam, on the other hand, rejected the advice of his father's trusted elders and instead surrounded himself with inexperienced, self-serving young men. From the beginning, they gave Rehoboam dreadful advice which

---

[9] Genesis 12:1-20.

resulted in dividing the kingdom of Israel. His poor choice of companions not only affected his own life, but the lives of generations to come.

Created for Companionship

In Ecclesiastes 4:9-10 we are reminded that "Two are better than one, because they have a good reward for their toil. For if they fall, one will lift up his fellow. But woe to him who is alone when he falls and has not another to lift him up!" Paul did not travel alone on his many journeys through Asia and the Mediterranean. He usually had a traveling companion, whether they were a co-worker in Christ such as Barnabas or Silas, or one of his students, Timothy, Titus, or Mark.

Luke was with Paul, often documenting his travels, and others, Epaphroditus, Tychicus, Onesimus, Aristarchus, Epaphras, Priscilla and Aquila came along to give encouragement, moral support, and prayer. Even Jesus knew He needed to surround Himself with loyal companions. Yes, He spent forty days alone in the desert, but when He emerged, He immediately began gathering men and women with whom He could share His deepest thoughts and teachings, and one day trust them to carry on the ministry of the Gospel.

143

Christ Our Constant Companion

There are times when traveling alone is necessary, to take that solitary walk, or pause if you will, to reflect on or contemplate our current situation. As Christians, however, we are not alone, for God promises to always be with us. In our journey through life, God does not desire for us to go it alone. Christ should be our constant companion through the ministry of the Holy Spirit. Christ desires to be with us as is evident in His discussion with His disciples of the vine and the branches in John 15:4-5. "Abide in me, and I in you. As the branch cannot bear fruit by itself, unless it abides in the vine, neither can you, unless you abide in me. I am the vine; you are the branches. Whoever abides in me and I in him, he it is that bears much fruit, for apart from me you can do nothing."

God does not intend for us to go on the journey of life alone. It is when we reach those long, lonely valleys in life, that we must remember the words of King David, "Even though I walk through the valley of the shadow of death, I will fear no evil, for you are with me; your rod and staff, they comfort me" (Psalm 23:4). We can rejoice, for God is our good shepherd who cares for our well-being.

The shepherd used the rod to guide, rescue, and protect his sheep, and his staff is a symbol of support.

When we journey through difficult times we can feel alone, abandoned, and scared. But God will not abandon you, neither will He ever forsake you or ignore the difficulties that you face. God promises to come alongside us to give guidance, comfort, and support. And there are days when the travel is wearisome and exhausting, not only physically, but emotionally draining to our spirit and soul. During those times remember God does not want us to bear the burden alone.

Jesus said, "Come to me, all you who are weary and burdened, and I will give you rest. Take my yoke upon you and learn from me, for I am gentle and humble in heart, and you will find rest for your souls. For my yoke is easy and my burden is light" (Matthew 11:28-30). We are all in need of both solitary moments, and times surrounded by friends and family. Our unique personalities and preferences mean we will each choose differently how much we travel alone or with companions, and unless one is a complete recluse, we will all be in relationship with others who will have a positive or negative influence on the decisions and paths we choose.

God Provides Relationships for our Good and Our Joy

From the beginning of time, God has said "It is not good for man to be alone" (Genesis 2:18). He has designed us to have need of one another whether in friendship, protection, accountability, instruction, comfort, procreation, or enjoyment. Clearly our most valued relationship should be between us and our heavenly Father. True joy comes from time spent with Him and in His Word, in meditation, prayer, and worship. He also intended for us to find joy as we are in relationship with one another. Consider the joy that comes from having a close friend to share life with, someone who can be there with you and for you, to laugh with and encourage you.

Ruth found that friendship in Naomi. Though they were mother- and daughter-in-law, they had formed a special bond. Ruth was even willing to leave her homeland to travel with Naomi and live with her. Ruth's dedication and commitment to Naomi later resulted in one of the most beautiful love stories in the Bible. Jonathan's commitment to his friendship with David was so deep, he was willing to defy his father, King Saul's wishes to protect David. Shadrach, Meshach, and Abednego served together under King Nebuchadnezzar in Babylon. They had to stick together and not compromise their faith while living in a

146

foreign land. Their friendship and their faith gave them the strength to stand up to the King, willing to face death. God honored their devotion and saved them from the fiery furnace. Paul and Silas traveled through Asia together sharing the Gospel, starting churches, and even going to prison together. Their willingness to serve God alongside one another was the beginning of the early church.

At other times, God brings others into our lives for accountability or training. "As iron sharpens iron, so one man sharpens another" (Proverbs 27:17). Clearly, God had placed Nathan the prophet into King David's trusted circle of advisors. At a critical time in David's reign, Nathan's rebuke and correction from God was the means to keeping David from his downfall. Through Nathan's relationship with David, God would guide and direct the most influential king of His kingdom.

Paul considered Timothy to be like a son. He took Timothy under his wing during his second missionary journey, and for the next fifteen years, Paul would mentor while Timothy would learn and go boldly with the encouragement of his friend and teacher. And Jesus, of course, spent most of his ministry in the company of his disciples, followers, and close friends. At times, Jesus' disciples didn't fully comprehend everything He taught

147

them, but they were more than mere students, they were His traveling companions, His friends and confidants, and His defenders as the world revolted against Him. Jesus' dearest friends, Mary, Martha, and Lazarus provided Him a friendship where He was free to express His very human emotions.

The Gift of One Another

The companionship of others is a gift from God, not to be taken lightly or carelessly. Yet, even as a gift, it is still up to us to pray and carefully choose whom we will travel with on this journey. We can choose to surround ourselves with those who distract us from the proper path, or those who will encourage and guide us in the right direction. We can choose those who will thwart our plans or those who will build us up. We can choose those who will bring us harm or those who will protect and defend us. And when God graciously brings good teachers, mentors, friends, and family into our lives, we should not push them away, but embrace them, for they may be our joy givers when difficulties make joy hard to find.

Who are your traveling companions? Who are your closest friends and confidants, your influencers? Do they have the freedom to pull you back on the path when you stray, to be honest with you? Do you have the freedom to call on them when you need encouragement, a good belly laugh, a shoulder to cry on, or refuge in the storm? Do you have someone who will pray with you or for you, or maybe who will sit with you, no words, just sit and be there for you? When it is in our power to do so, we must carefully choose with whom we will travel.

Lord help me to choose carefully
my friends along the way,
To journey with companions
that encourage, teach and pray.
Whether the path is lonely,
or filled with many friends,
I know that you are with me,
on your presence I depend.

Ten

Extra Baggage and Dirty Laundry

"Get rid of all bitterness, rage and anger, brawling and
slander, along with every form of malice. Be kind and
compassionate to one another, forgiving each other,
just as in Christ God forgave you"
Ephesians 4:31-32

Unpacking the Baggage

Have you ever seen the *Long, Long Trailer* with
Lucille Ball? Lucy and Desi take this fantastic honeymoon
trip across the country to their new home, pulling a long
travel trailer. Lucy obsesses with collecting a rock from
every... and I mean every, place they stop! The movie
depicts a hysterical comedy of errors as the trailer becomes
weighed down with hundreds of pounds of rocks. The
uphill climbs were slow, the downhill out of control. And
all because the unnecessary weight was added to the
journey.

Oftentimes, while traveling, we collect an assortment of souvenirs and gifts. By the end of the trip, they begin to weigh us down and we barely have room to squeeze them into our luggage. Once home we distribute the items or throw them away, otherwise, they will collect dust and perhaps even litter our path. In our own lives, we collect an assortment of habits, emotions, and activities that can clutter and weigh us down. We end up with extra baggage and the unnecessary things in our lives need unloading.

Paul continually reminded the early church that having proper motives and attitudes was essential to abundant life in Christ. In his letter to the Colossians he said, "Put to death whatever belongs to your earthly nature" (Colossians 3:5) and instead "clothe yourselves with compassion, kindness, humility, gentleness and patience." (Colossians 3:12). When we do these things there will be peace, rejoicing, and gratitude in our hearts (Colossians 3:15-16). The book of Hebrews also admonishes with this, "let us throw off everything that hinders and the sin that so easily entangles and let us run with perseverance the race made out before us" (Hebrews 12:1).

Doing this requires, that on occasion, we take inventory of the attitudes and habits we have picked up along our journey, whether good or bad. What attitudes should we toss out because they cause clutter and breed destruction? Col. 3:8 warns us, "But now you must rid yourselves of all such things as these: anger, rage, malice, slander, and filthy language from your lips." Are you holding on to bitterness from a broken relationship? Do you experience envy because your friends seem to have an easy journey? Do you keep an account of those who have wronged you? Are you holding on to pride? *Get rid of it*! Don't allow such things to weigh you down on your journey and rob you of your joy.

Once we have emptied the unnecessary baggage, we are now able to focus on the good which has been collected. When we find a wonderful memento on our trip, we want to bring it out and display it. What good habits or qualities have you gained along the way worth displaying? Remember those things Paul mentioned in Colossians 3:12? We are to put on or display those qualities in our lives for all the world to see as a testimony of God's grace in our lives. In this way, the world will see you journey with joy rather than fear, distress, and bitterness in your heart. Have your travels helped you find patience with others or compassion for a neighbor? Are you now more forgiving because of how many times you have needed to be forgiven? Be sure to unpack your attitudes and habits on a regular basis, throwing out the bad and displaying the good.

Dirty Laundry

Keeping up with the laundry is a weekly routine, but when we return from a trip, occasionally the amount we bring home is overwhelming. The massive mound of laundry seems never ending and keeps us from getting back to our regular routine. While some of the things in our lives do need to be completely thrown out, like the unnecessary items collected along the journey, some areas in our lives may simply need a good cleaning. If we were to fold up our dirty laundry without washing it, put it back in the drawer, and wear it over and over again, it would eventually begin to stink and the stains would show, adversely affecting all those around us. We should, of course, daily come before our heavenly Father with confession and repentance, yet there are times when our lives are piled high with the dirty laundry of our transgressions, requiring some serious deep cleaning to effectively get the stains out.

Do we need to clean out the sarcasm or gossip in our talk? "Keep your heart with all vigilance, for from it flow the springs of life. Put away from you crooked speech, and put devious talk far from you" (Proverbs 4:23-24) Is there a relationship with family or friends, a spouse, co-worker, or neighbor requiring mending or restoration? (Colossians 3:13) What is the content of the movies, television, and entertainment that you allow into your home? (Philippians 4:8) Is it honoring to God? Psalm 51:10-12 says, "Create in me a clean heart, O God, and renew a right spirit within me. Cast me not away from your presence, and take not your Holy Spirit from me. Restore to me the joy of your salvation, and uphold me with a willing spirit." You see, our soiled laundry diminishes the beauty of our God-given wardrobe, keeping others from seeing who we are in Christ.

When not dealt with, the piles begin to grow, and we become overwhelmed with the burden. Deep soul searching and confessions are sometimes required to remove the stains and the sin in our lives. "If we say we have no sin, we deceive ourselves, and the truth is not in us. If we confess our sins, he is faithful and just to forgive us our sins and cleanse us from all unrighteousness" (1 John 1:8-9). Once we have cleaned the dirty laundry of our sin, our hearts are clean. When our hearts are clean and pure before God, we are then able to rejoice once more.

We do not live perfect lives, and we are not on a perfect journey. There will always be extra baggage and dirty laundry in our lives. However, we need not carry it forever. This is why Christ, in His journey, laid down His life and rose again so we would not have to bear the burden of our sin. Are we willing to let go and throw out the unnecessary baggage and confess those things in our lives which need the deep cleaning of Christ's redemptive blood? None of us wants to travel with extra weight and dirty clothes. A joyful journey is one free of burden and shame, so give them to God one bag, one pile at a time, and then rejoice with a spring in your step!

When I wonder why the road is rough,
Could it be I have too much stuff?
Some attitudes I think I know,
Are not so good and need to go.
Sometimes I need to cleanse my heart,
Rejoicing when I have a fresh start.
A joyful way I can be sure,
When before God, my heart is pure.

Eleven

How Long is Our Journey?

"Man's days are determined; you have decreed the number
of his months and have set limits he cannot exceed"

Job 14:5

We are all given a road to walk on. What we do not
know is how long our road or journey will be. We have
hopes and dreams for ourselves and our loved ones for a
long and fulfilling life. However, not everyone's journey
will be the same. Some will be short, as in the two-day-old
infant who succumbs to a birth defect, a teenager's life cut
short by a drunk driver, or a young adult who dies too early
from cancer. Others, however, may live a long, eventful life
well into their 80s or 90s before their journey ends. Though
we do not know the number of days God has determined
for our journey, we should know that it does matter how we
travel the road we walk on, whether short or long.

Stephen was a man full of faith and the Holy Spirit.
A young man when named as a deacon, his ministry and

influence grew quickly. God could have used a man of his stature to do many great things. God, however, chose to be glorified through his death and martyrdom. Stephen's life was short, yet he praised God to the very end, and his death still impacts the church to this day.

I was blessed to know a young man, Clayton McDonald, who had a profound impact on his community even though he only lived eighteen precious years. His diagnosis of Leukemia came at the age of seven. His parents and siblings rallied around him through chemotherapy treatments, two bone marrow transplants, and passing in and out of remission three times. His church and community prayed for him and came alongside the family. What was most remarkable about Clayton was his faith and devotion to God in the face of death. Because he had the assurance of one day being with his Savior, he was not as concerned about his own death as he was for the souls of others, especially teens.

He, like the Apostle Paul, saw dying as gain but did not want to leave this earth until he could share the Gospel with as many as possible. In his final months on this earth, he spoke at churches and youth events, sharing the urgency of knowing and believing in Christ. Only five days before his passing he spoke at Cal Poly San Luis Obispo to over

900 of his peers. Many teens and adults came to Christ because of his commitment to sharing the Gospel. Clayton invested in the lives of others and had an incredible way of connecting with his peers and all those he encountered. After graduating high school, he enjoyed working with junior high students at his church and was even able to go on a mission trip to Costa Rica.

For a young man of eighteen, he was loved and respected by many. Clayton had people praying for him from all over the world because they were so inspired by his story and his passion for the lost. The night before the Lord took him home, he asked his closest friends to come to his house. As they sat in a circle, he proceeded to speak to each one, sharing the impact they had had on his life, praying for them, and encouraging them to fight the good fight.

That, to me, is one of the finest examples of putting others before oneself. He had a great love for the people around him, yet his love for God was even greater still. Clayton's road in this life was short, but he walked it with tremendous purpose and with more grace and courage than most of us will in a lifetime. He found a joy in life that most of us might miss, and his story is a beautiful testimony of true devotion to God.

In both examples, Stephen and Clayton traveled their short journeys with great passion. Others have traveled long, and oftentimes, difficult roads with equal passion. Noah spent years being taunted as he built a boat that seemed foolish to all those around. But he did not stop trusting God and continued building. When Noah was 600 years old, God sent the flood waters, using Noah and his family to save humanity and the earth from total and complete destruction.

God rewarded Noah's steadfastness with a covenant promise to never flood the entire earth again and then proceeded to replenish the earth with His creation. Simeon was a very old man when he finally met the Christ child at the temple. The Holy Spirit had promised Simeon he would not die until he had seen Christ. When he did, he rejoiced and prophesied over the Christ child. God had purposed Simeon to live a long and devoted life to Him for this very reason, to glorify God.

Consider the life of Corrie Ten Boom. During her 91-year journey, she faced heartache and devastating trials. She had devoted herself to the ministry of those in need, the guidance and instruction of young girls, and working alongside her father. In 1940 the war changed everything about her world, and it was then that their ministry changed to offering refuge to the Jews and others who were hunted by the Gestapo. In 1944 Corrie and her family were imprisoned in the Nazi concentration camps where she endured unspeakable atrocities while her father and sister died in the camps.

She had complete trust God knew what He was doing. She understood how she responded to those trials is what would define her ministry, lasting another four decades. A verse that gave Corrie great hope while in the concentration camp was 1 Peter 4:12, "Beloved, do not be surprised at the fiery trial when it comes upon you to test you, as though something strange were happening to you. But rejoice insofar as you share Christ's suffering, that you may also rejoice and be glad when his glory is revealed."

She, like Paul, found joy despite the circumstances. The ministry following her imprisonment brought hope and the Gospel to countless individuals in over sixty countries. She wrote over thirty books and inspired many as she spoke with joy and thankfulness for the life God had called her to. It is difficult to imagine her joy and passion for Christ came out of a life filled with suffering and pain. She once said, "This is what the past is for! Every experience God gives us, every person He puts in our lives is the perfect preparation for the future that only He can see[10]." This is a good reminder, for whatever circumstance we face on life's road, God can and will use it for His glory, and in that we can ultimately rejoice.

For most of us, the length of our journey will fall somewhere in between the brief life of Clayton and the 91 years of Corrie Ten Boom. Regardless of how short or long your journey is, what will your legacy be? How will you look back on your life, how will you be remembered? Will we, like Paul, be able to say, "I have fought the good fight, I have finished the race, I have kept the faith" (2 Timothy 4:7). I hope I am not remembered as a quarrelsome wife, frustrated mom, or complaining co-worker.

Did I put the interest of others before myself? Was my life's work or ministry self-serving or God-honoring? My hope is that my faith in Christ leaves a legacy of joy and pleasure to those who knew me, and my life will be a reflection of God's love and mercy, goodness, and grace. Joy is, after all, a fruit of the Spirit and if our life-long goal is to be like Christ and filled with the Spirit, then joy unspeakable and full of glory, as the old hymn says, should be reflected in our life's journey, our legacy.

---

[10] *The Hiding Place* by Corrie tenBoom with John and Elizabeth Sherrill. Used by permission of Chosen Books LLC.

I do not know the length of days

for this journey I am on.

How will I be remembered

when this fleeting life is gone

Will those who walked beside me

be encouraged by my faith

And in my chance encounters

have I kindly shown God's grace

Will my testimony bring Him Glory

when my days are done

Whatever days are given me,

has joy been in each one?

Twelve

Keeping a Record

"Let this be written for a future generation,
that a people not yet created may praise the LORD"
Psalm 102:18

When I sat down to write this final chapter, we were finishing up a short winter trip to the mountains. I watched out the window as the first real snowfall of the season turned everything into a winter wonderland. At the end of the trip, I posted some pictures on social media to record the memories and the fun.

How do you remember what you did on a trip or vacation? When we take a vacation, we often record the events through pictures, videos, or journals. As we travel through life, we can also keep a record of how we have been blessed, how we have persevered, what we have learned and how we served God and others.

When Joshua finally led the Israelites across the Jordan, God commanded each tribe to take large stones

163

from the middle of the Jordan and place them as memorial stones before the priests. God wanted the Israelites to remember what He had done in delivering them and bringing them into the Promised Land. Would we know of God's wondrous works, of His plan of redemption, of His love and mercies, if not for the scribes and writers of God's Holy Word? God wants us to remember and proclaim His mercies and His mighty works by keeping a record. How can we do this? There are tools we can use which will help us to keep an account of what God has done in our lives, as a way of passing on encouragement, teaching, and wisdom to future generations.

Journals

On our trip to Indiana, I had our then seven-year-old daughter keep a journal of our trip, complete with illustrations. We pull it out every so often to enjoy again, and now her journal has become a treasured heirloom. I have gone through intermittent periods in my life of keeping journals. Journal writing has been a common form of record-keeping for centuries. In the late-1900s it gradually became a lost art with the advent of technology in television, computers, and cell phones.

There has been, however, a resurgence of journaling in the form of blogs and other forms of social media. Many are even keeping handwritten journals again or writing a daily log on their computer. Whatever form you choose, keeping a journal of some kind can be a treasured possession, bringing joy to a child or grandchild one day. And when you occasionally read through a passage you have written you may learn something about yourself or be encouraged by what God has done on your journey.

The most extraordinary journal of all is the one written by God, His Word, from creation to revelation! We can rejoice and be grateful when we read with the understanding that God's Word is His story, and the testimonies and narratives reveal to each generation who He is, His character, His glory, and His plan of redemption. Even more remarkable to me, is when we realize our story is woven into His story. His Word has unveiled His past glories, and when we tell our own stories of how His love and redemption impacted our lives, we will also reveal His glory.

Answered Prayer

Do you keep a prayer list? How often do you go back and make note of how God answered those prayer requests? God does answer prayer, sometimes with yes, other times with no or wait, and sometimes in ways we would never expect. What a joy to experience God's personal involvement in our journey through life. Remember those nine months my husband was out of work? It was during this time we decided to keep a list of answered prayers and how God provided for our needs in ways we never imagined.

The list was extensive. At times there were little things like a small, but meaningful note of encouragement. At other times an anonymous envelope appeared with exactly the amount of money we needed to pay a bill. It was incredible to read over the list and humbly be in awe of how God met our daily needs through prayer and His people. There is much joy in answered prayer!

I will give thanks to the LORD with my whole heart; I will recount all of your wonderful deeds.
I will be glad and exult in you; I will sing praise to your name, O Most High."
Psalm 9:1-2

Letters

Much of America's early history is known in part because of the letters written by our country's founders and

166

leaders such as William Bradford, one of the original settlers, and first governor of the Plymouth Colony. He, along with other early settlers, wrote letters and kept extensive journals describing the land, the people, the establishment of government, along with their hardships and accomplishments. John and Abigail Adams' wrote letters to each other filled with tremendous detail about the White House and the office of the Presidency during America's infancy. Today, some families follow the tradition of writing an annual family letter at Christmas or for the New Year. Unfortunately, letter writing has also become a lost art. I love getting letters. There is something about unfolding the card or piece of stationery in anticipation, reading with piqued interest, and soaking in bits of information or kind, encouraging words. When done I fold it up again and the effort seems to give its contents more value, and more meaning.

I admit, I wish I were better with the frequency of my letter writing. I also enjoy reading our own letters from years past and being reminded of what God did each year and what was important to us then. The ritual helps me to remember if those were joyful or anxious years. How well did we travel life back then? And, again, we rediscover what God did and what we learned.

The letters Paul wrote to the churches and to Timothy have become powerful words of encouragement for a Christian's walk. If you have rarely or never sat down to write a thoughtful letter, you might want to consider taking up letter writing, whether it be an annual letter to family and friends, love letters to your sweetheart, children or grandchildren, or letters to good friends who have moved away. It is a hobby that will not disappoint.

God wants us to reflect and remember the past, not dwell on or get lost in it, but learn from the past and rejoice in it. In 1 Chronicles 16:8-12, David wrote this Psalm:

> "Give praise to the LORD, proclaim his name; make known among the nations what he has done. Sing to him, sing praise to him; tell of all his wonderful acts. Glory in his holy name; let the hearts of those who seek the LORD rejoice. Look to the LORD and his strength; seek his face always. Remember the wonders he has done, his miracles and the judgments he pronounced" (Psalm 105:1-5).

And even earlier, we see that in Psalm 77, David also says:

> "I will remember the deeds of the LORD; yes, I will remember your miracles of long

ago. I will consider all your works and

meditate on all your mighty deeds"

(Psalm 77:11-12)

We will better remember when we keep a record of
what God has done. As we endeavor to travel this journey
with joy, we should desire to share with others the source
of our joy: God and his son Jesus Christ. I would encourage
you to find ways to keep a record of all the marvelous ways
God has worked in your life's journey, to leave a legacy of
joy for future generations. Don't be silent or too timid to
tell your story. Through the stories of each of our
individual journeys, God's glory is remembered and
revealed.

Your wondrous works have been recorded

for all the world to see.

May I not forget to share

the things you've done for me.

My life is filled with joy because

of forgiveness and your grace,

So may I boldly tell of you

when going place to place.

Epilogue

Joy in the Journey

My desire is that the words on these pages have inspired and encouraged you to find or continue with joy as you walk along life's road. I have come to realize we often desire happiness, but God wants us to experience joy, pure and abiding joy. The journey of writing this has been an eye-opener for me. Though I have generally had a positive, joyful outlook on life, there were definitely stages in my journey that were not joyous and certainly not a reflection of God's love and mercy. Times of rebellion as a young adult, over-commitment, and discontentment as a young mom and wife caused me to misplace my joy in the Lord which adversely affected my relationship with God, my family, and my friends. Yet, over time, God has gently shown me these beautiful lessons of how to experience His joy every day, in every circumstance.

Do I still fall into discontentment, discouragement, and sorrow? Yes, but considerably less often, and I have allowed God to pull me back into His loving embrace much sooner than I would have in the past. I only wish I had followed more of these principles earlier in my journey and not missed out on the joy which was freely available to me. My prayer is wherever you are in your journey you will not allow another moment to go by without a daily dose of God's joy to brighten each step. James tells us, "Draw near to God, and he will draw near to you." (James 4:8) We do this through prayer, meditating on scripture, and fellowship with other Christians. When we truly abide in Christ, we will experience and exhibit the sweet joy which comes from the Holy Spirit.

God has placed us all on a journey and He desires for us to experience joy whether traveling the beaten path or on the detours of life. He doesn't want us to get so caught up in arriving at our destination that we miss the beauty and joy of life along the way. Seeking God's wisdom and being in a close and abiding relationship with God is key to keeping joy in our lives. Prayer, trust, and obedience are essential, especially when the trials of life throw us off the path, lead us through a dark tunnel, or take us across a long or wobbly bridge. Every steppingstone in life has a purpose, and we can trust God to faithfully guide us on the sure and steady path. He will also come alongside, correcting and disciplining us when we have veered from the path.

There will be testing, suffering and valuable lessons to be learned, and each trial brings God glory, He merely asks us to be faithful and rejoice in His sovereignty and goodness. Find and embrace your best traveling companions, ones who will be your joy givers, building you up with support, protection, and guidance. We do not know how long our journey will be, but we do know God desires for us to be steadfast in joy, regardless of the circumstances. "Rejoice in the Lord always, I will say it again: Rejoice!" (Philippians 4:4). Our joy is not contingent on how we feel, but on the attitude of our heart toward God and His promises. As you walk the road God has set before you, remember His grace and mercy toward you, declaring His faithfulness by living a joy-filled life where God is the source of contentment, peace, and joy.

"You make known to me the path of life; in your presence there is fullness of joy; at your right hand are pleasures forevermore." - Psalm 16:11

The Road We Walk On

Sometimes the road we walk on
    seems so sure and firm.
There is no fear what lies ahead
    or what's beyond the turn.
We make our plans, we walk along,
    certain of our goal.
The way seems sure, the way seems firm
    as we walk along the road.
        So, if we have it all planned out
      why does the road get rough?
      We don't expect the twists and turns
      that make the journey tough.
      We come upon a roadblock
    or detour on the way,
      And all the plans we thought so sure
    can change in just a day.
If on the road we stumble
    His steady hand is firm,
To pick us up and guide us
    on the road that we should turn.

We may not clearly see the road

on dark and dreary days,

Yet when we put our trust in God,

He illuminates our ways.

Remember our steps are marked out by God,

He knows what lies ahead.

He knows the plans He has for us

we need not fear nor dread.

So, when the road we walk on

takes us to a different place,

We forge ahead, we trust His plan

in the journey we now face.

And as we walk upon each road

facing trials along the way,

He gives us strength to stand the test

His joy our hope and stay.

He makes known to us the path of life

until our days are done,

In His presence there is fullness of joy

for this road we walk upon.

Acknowledgments

I have been writing since I was a young girl. First short stories, then poems. During my years of homeschooling and in children's ministry, I even wrote the curriculum for my students. Then in 2010, as I attended a women's conference, I was convicted of the lack of true joy in my life, God's joy. I began to study and meditate on the many nuances of joy, and all these stories and analogies constantly filled my mind and my heart. And so, the foundation of what I didn't know would eventually become a book, was formed.

There have been many rewrites, additions, and subtractions since this journey began, and I could not have accomplished this without several sweet friends, mentors, and family to walk along this road with me. They provided me with encouragement, constructive critiques, motivation, direction, and much, much prayer!

Phil – my dear, patient husband, you have supported and encouraged me in this endeavor, even when a writing binge meant I forgot to make dinner or finish the laundry! Thank you for reading through each draft and version and giving your honest and valuable suggestions. You are my rock and my lifelong companion on our journey together as cohorts and best friends. You are one of the greatest joys of my life.

Sarah, Nathan, Andrew, and Joshua – being your mom has been a joy and blessing, and my mind is filled with the memories of fun adventures, learning, and curiosity. Although it became my job to teach and mold each of you as we home-schooled, I can truly say you have taught me so much more than I ever imagined through your own journeys of faith, triumphs, challenges, struggles, and accomplishments. I love you and the beautiful families you have created, and the source of much of my joy in this life! Sarah, thank you for using your creative gifts to design the beautiful cover for my book.

Joseph Bentz – You have been an invaluable resource to me both as a mentor and an encourager. Your experience as a literature professor and a fellow writer with several books under your belt has provided me with an excellent example of how to glorify God in my writing with patience, perseverance, humility, and excellence. Thank you for encouraging me to expand my first draft and patiently critiquing key passages of my manuscript.

Karen Goertzen – as one of my dearest friends you had a profound impact on how I would learn to view life with the heart and compassion of Jesus, rejoice with an attitude of Paul, and serve God with perseverance and diligence. You faithfully walked with me, teaching me the art of ministry life. You patiently listened when I talked, then you shared your pearls of wisdom, and I was often left humbled yet grateful to have a friend who spoke truth to me with love and grace. Much of what God has taught me about joy and rejoicing was done through you by your example, mentoring, and friendship. Thank you for reading my manuscript many times over and giving your advice and encouragement to see this to completion.

Pastor Ron and Susie Johnson – Thank you for helping me keep this book theologically sound and true to God's Word. I have learned and profited tremendously from your teaching, and maybe even picked up a few storytelling techniques along the way. You and Susie have been an incredible example of how to "count it all joy" in the challenges of this life. You have also been a great source of encouragement to me in ministry and my writing. Susie, thank you for allowing me to share a small glimpse of your cancer journey.

Julie Walker, Sharyn Dike, and Kathy Ide – you each played a significant part in keeping me from rambling, making grammatical faux pas, and helping my writing style to be readable. Julie, thank you for reading through and giving feedback on my first drafts. Sharyn, thank you for proofreading my manuscript and finding all the little things the rest of us miss. Julie and Sharyn, I am also grateful for your words of encouragement, prayer, and longstanding friendships. Kathy, thank you for writing *Editing Secrets of Best-Selling Authors*[11]. It was the perfect resource to help me clean up my final drafts and put a smile on my editor's face. I am grateful to have met and worked with you at our last writer's retreat.

Wendy McDonald – Thank you for the honor and joy of sharing your precious son's story. Clayton was a remarkable young man. I only had the privilege of crossing his path a handful of times, but each time I walked away in awe of his maturity in Christ, and his enthusiasm for life in the face of an uncertain future. Though his life was short, he left an indelible mark on the world and a wonderful example of living a life for Christ with joy.

---

[11] Editing Secrets of Best-Selling Authors, by Kathy Ide, 2020.

My Women's Ministry Team at Village Bible Church — It has been a joy and privilege to lead and serve alongside each one of you. Your prayers, encouragement, and friendship have meant the world to me. You have been examples of how to walk through life as godly women, serving the body of Christ with humility, compassion, and joy.

My long-time friends, fellow writers, and prayer warriors — Cookie, Sharon, Joy, Donna, Debbi, JoAnne, Susy, and a handful of others — you have patiently listened to me dream about my first book, encouraged me when I wondered if it was ever going to happen, prayed for me in both my life and my writing endeavors. Thank you for being there with your words of encouragement, advice, knowledge, and wisdom.

Adam Lowe — you were a God send! When I finally realized I was in the final stages of making this a reality, then came the technical part of writing I do not look forward to: final edits, finding and citing permissions, formatting and publication. God's timing was perfect. Just when I needed someone with your expertise, your schedule became available, and you were the brilliant compliment to my writing style, and to understanding my vision. You were exactly what I needed to complete the journey of writing and publishing this book in a way that would bring glory and honor to God Almighty!

About the Author

Janene is joyfully married to her husband, Phil, of 38 years. They have 4 grown children, 5 grandchildren, and one on the way. Janene has had a love for writing since elementary school, whether it be short stories, sports journalism, or poetry. She was a home-schooling mom for 24 years and Children's Church Director for over 15 years, giving her opportunities to write curriculum for their homeschool co-op and children's church.

For the past 16 years and counting, Janene has been the Women's Ministry Director of her church. She has written over 100 poems and a handful of children's short stories. Janene loves words and loves to tell a story, whether fiction or non-fiction. Her journey has finally brought her to a season in life where those words can now become books and bring joy to others.

Made in the USA
Las Vegas, NV
17 March 2024

87348095R00105